D0231354

Who Really Killed
Cock Robin?

BY THE SAME AUTHOR

A Pagan Funeral
When the Warm Times Come
Seeing What I Mean
Messages From the Museums of Man

Some of the restorations in this volume have previously appeared in private publications:
The Pagan Carols Restored
The Nursery Rhymes Restored To Their Adult Originals
The Resurrection Of Cock Robin

NORMAN ILES

Who Really Killed Cock Robin?

NURSERY RHYMES AND CAROLS RESTORED TO THEIR ORIGINAL MEANINGS

Illustrations by Harry Iles

ROBERT HALE · LONDON

© *This collection Norman Iles 1986*
Illustrations © Harry Iles 1986
First published in Great Britain 1986

Iles, Norman
    Who really killed Cock Robin? : nursery
    rhymes and carols restored to their
    original pagan meanings.
    1. Folk poetry, English——History and
    criticism   2. English poetry——History and
    criticism
    I. Title
    398'.8   PR507

ISBN 0–7090–2630–7

Robert Hale Limited
Clerkenwell House
Clerkenwell Green
London EC1 R 0HT

Set in Walbaum by Kelly Typesetting Ltd., Bradford on Avon.
Printed in Great Britain by St. Edmundsbury Press, Bury St.
Edmunds, Suffolk and bound by Woolnough.

Contents

CAROLS   **119**

Carol tunes not given here are in the *Oxford Book of Carols.*

Acknowledgements

First, to Tom Wakefield, 'Forties Child', who helped me, a Sixties Child, enliven the prose of the earlier *Resurrection of Cock Robin*. He wouldn't let it hide its head under its wing, poor thing, but helped it put out its horns and crow!

Then, to the source-book of almost all my quotations, *The Oxford Dictionary of Nursery Rhymes*, edited by Iona and Peter Opie (Oxford University Press, 1951). Although my interpretations are far from theirs, I do acknowledge the debt I owe them for their care of the nursery rhymes' texts, their finding of other versions, and their notes.

Nursery Rhymes

'I very much want to put into the world again the big, old pagan vision, before the idea and the concept of personality made everything so small and tight as it is now,' D. H. LAWRENCE, letter.

'The distortion of a text is not unlike a murder. The difficulty lies not in the execution of the deed but in doing away with the traces ... That is why, in so many textual distortions, we may count on finding the suppressed material hidden away somewhere, though in an altered shape, and torn out of its original connection.' FREUD, *Moses and Monotheism.*

'For double the vision my eyes do see,
And a double vision is always with me.'
                                        WILLIAM BLAKE

9

How do you do? An introduction

I have discovered the repository of sexual folk-verse. It is called *The Oxford Dictionary of Nursery Rhymes*. The sexual verses, having had the sense knocked out of them, and their form deranged, became infantile. Arranged alphabetically, they are presented to children.

My work is to restore them to their original forms, and to prove my restorations correct. I begin each reconstruction by quoting the rhyme given in *The Oxford Dictionary of Nursery Rhymes* (ODNR) as the standard text. Then I quote any other versions I find relevant. From this source material, I deduce where changes were made, and how to rectify them. Then I produce the restored rhyme.

It is acknowledged that the great majority of the rhymes were not composed for children. 'In fact, many are survivals of an adult code of joviality, and, in their original wording, were, by present standards, strikingly unsuitable for those of tender years' (ODNR). Yet those strikingly unsuitable originals are rarely to be found amongst the versions. Usually, there is no documented degeneration from the first adult joke to the present nursery rhyme. All the versions are fragmented and confused.

The reason is clear. Strikingly unsuitable adult jokes could not be published before the obscenity laws were relaxed in 1963. What could be printed before then, were bowdlerized versions or incomplete ones. Those who prefer nonsense jingles, pretty trifles, to sexual verses, have been content to leave them like that.

As the subject matter was not permissible in polite

society, those who knew the words changed them if they were in the company of the rich, the respectable and the learned. A folk-singer told Cecil Sharp, who usually collected songs with the help of the local vicar, that such verses were 'way-out rude'. What is 'adult joviality' but a euphemism, a bowdlerization?

Consequently, the symbolism became harder to understand, at the very time that realism and science were becoming dominant in our culture. The very pub signs are now taken realistically, as if the Black Bull meant merely a dark, male cow, and the Game Cock Inn was a public house where fighting-cocks drank! Folk-speech, rhyme and song have always seen human resemblances in their surroundings. 'Empty barrels make the most sound' has very little to do with barrels and very much to do with people. For the under-meaning is the important one in symbolism. Today, teachers have to explain proverbs to children. Our culture has been disrupted. Men no longer smile secretly when they enter the Dun Cow.

The present reaction against sexual repression, because it is matter-of-fact, has been unable to comprehend the symbolism of the past. It is that culture-gap which I am trying to bridge. Only the most working-class members of the working-class, the rejected and rejecting, still use the old imagery. Only in a lower-class pub will a man say 'Here's lead in your pencil!' Only in a market have I heard a woman say, about a wife leaving her husband, 'Starvation drives away the cat, satisfaction brings her back.' The result is that rhymes with cats in, or bullets made of 'lead, lead, lead', are being taken literally—as if the market-woman were teaching elementary zoology.

What we have to realize is, that if we are fortunate enough to hear someone sing 'Little Tommy Tucker, Poor little fucker'; or

> There was a ram of Derbyshire
> Who had three horns of brass
> And two grew out of his head, sir
> And one grew out of his arse,

we are not hearing modern parodies which must instantly be shut out of our superior minds. For Tommy is not a little child (though he may be unfortunate), and the great ram of Derby was a fertility symbol, and his third horn had to be of brass, symbolically. Half-remembered, he still stands over Derby County's football ground, because men used to like to project themselves as rams—and as Rovers and as Hot Spurs.

'Little' is like 'old'. Both are wrongly defined by the single vision which has no depth of field. They are terms of familiarity, not of flat fact. 'My old woman' does not mean my wife is old. 'A little man who does carpentry' is not a dwarf. So Old Mother Hubbard is not automatically excluded from a sexual happening. Little Bo-Peep is big enough to have two teen-age daughters. Somehow, realism influences us more when we read than when we talk, for in everyday speech we do understand such simple second meanings.

Comprehension of imagery is my method, not seeking for more sources. I hope the ODNR has done the textual research for me. From all its versions, I try to understand the hidden, partial story. It's like trying to decode a message, which is often incomplete. But people, very realistic people, do restore confused messages. They call their work Intelligence. It is reconstruction by deduction, not by production of a new-found manuscript pasted in the back of a cookery-book, dated 1066 and signed W.C. Its proof is from its sources, its logic, its unity. It makes sense where there was no sense. But circumstantial evidence is found less convincing, today, than factual evidence. We distrust our powers of thought; but only thought can decide between two versions which are equally authentic and almost equally old. Interpretations can be wrong, but I do not see how they can do harm. The versions still exist, to disprove or approve, them.

Often sung in our Folk Club was

This couple agreed and were married with speed,
And away to the church they did go.

I approached the singer and said, if they were married, need they go away to church? I suggested 'their bed'. But he went on singing 'church'. He was conservative and he likes church. But . . .

'Do not think what you want to think before you know what you ought to know,' says my favourite spy-book.* The knowledge we want is folk-knowledge. All the slang, jokes, rugby songs, writing on lavatory walls; all the odd, old sayings; all customs, pub. signs, patterns; the art in folk museums, the carvings in old churches. All these are from the same folk culture and relate to the rhymes and carols. Books on them may, or may not, be enlightening. What you ought to know you may have to find out for yourself. The authoritative book may be wrong. Doubt it. People began with the Bible.

Let us begin with the names. Many rhymes have a main character whose naming begins them. How many of them are 'little' or 'old'! There are Humpty Dumpty, Bo-Peep, Miss Muffet, Old Roger, Dicky Delver, Jack Horner. All those names are

---

* *Most Secret War*, by R. V. Jones (Coronet Books)

14

meaningful, once they're seen as metaphor, once we've woken up to double meaning. They personify Miss Short-and-Broad, Ms In-and-Out, Miss Little Muff, John Thomas, Dicky Digger, Jack Horn-er. Do we forget the way Shakespeare called his characters Toby Belch, Mistress Quickly, Doll Tearsheet? I'm sure teachers are careful not to explain those to pupils. Each is a type, a simplification, whose name is him in deed. The folk wanted to tell what happened to these types as examples of what will happen if someone behaves as they did:

All the king's horses,
All the king's men
Couldn't put that short-and-broad girl together again.

Having found a general, human meaning in the rhymes, I did not find a particular historic realism in them. The historical interpretation of nursery rhymes has served to stop the search for other meaning. Somehow they would be understood if only we knew more of some event dim in history. The two best known examples of historical interpretation are of 'Three Blind Mice' and 'Ring, A Ring O' Roses'. But the farmer's wife cannot be the wife of Farmer George, courted by three 'blind' noblemen, for the very historical reason that the first version dates from before the Georges. The 'ring o' roses' cannot refer to the plague-rash, because another version carries the song on to 'The wedding bells are ringing.' The fact that people go on repeating rhymes long after the supposed event, long after its effects have died away, shows the improbability of historical meaning. Some of these rhymes have European equivalents. Very few historical events have deeply affected all the peoples of Europe. But events which are not historical, but everyday, would affect them all—things like birth, marriage and death—and they'd be rhymes that people would repeat like proverbs. Why should people want to remember some queen's doings or misdoings for hundreds of years? But general sexual behaviour, adult joviality, that might survive from the version of 1609:

"Three blind mice, three blind mice,
. . . The Miller and his merry old wife,
She scraped her tripe, lick thou the knife."

Somewhen, meaning, like that, has been lost or destroyed. Realistic and scientific though we are, if a whole metaphorical verse is published, some of us do understand it. So, suppression and alteration have been used to break the wholeness. Nearly always, the beginning is still the original one, because it is only the beginning. But, when meaning is being defined, then the story is turned. Fortunately, inevitably, that wrong turning must be shown by cracks in the logic of the narrative, and in its form. No poem, no song or carol, can have its meaning changed without trace. If the alteration were done very carefully, the trace would be faint, and the difficulty of proof great. My prose would have to argue on for pages, and proof would depend on fine points of understanding and form. But usually the suppressor, or the forgetter, is not as careful as the composer. He only wants to make passable verse, because his purpose is social and moral, not poetic. He has contemporary society on his side, so there will be ready acceptance, and publication, of his changes. He will not fear confrontation from the peasants. Big Brother has watched over the flock many times. As for the forgetter, the first thing that comes to his mind will do. Singers who forget their words at a Folk Club often repeat those of a previous verse or jump to the next one. If they invent,

16

both usually lose rhyme or rhythm or grammar or verse-form. It's difficult to find another rhyme which makes sense, difficult to find sense that scans, difficult to compose a new verse that fits. Because of these difficulties, a common way of censoring is simply to omit the troublesome part. But that must cause a break in the sense of the poem, and sometimes it comes too late, after a written record has been made.

Another simple way of disguising the meaning is to change the sex of the participants. If a man does what a woman should do, it makes quite a perversion of the sense. In the ODNR standard text of 'White Bird Featherless' it is Lord Landless who takes up, 'handless', the phallic symbol—to the confusion of all. But an earlier version gives 'Wife Mouthless', and all is normally ordered again. 'Jack and Jill' was once presented as a rhyme about two boys! To write 'he' instead of 'she' is the quickest way to censor, and it's surprisingly effective. Holly and Ivy carols are censored by calling holly 'she'.

The bad joinings reveal, even as they conceal— once one is looking for bad joinings. They mark the spot, make the doubter look and think. They suggest, by their approximation, what the original was.

Restoration rises from the determination to make the rhyme live again. No one would restore something he did not believe was better than the counterfeit. In fact, the nursery rhymes are dying, after having been, in their original form, alive for hundreds of years. The ODNR lists 550 rhymes, but most are now unsaid, unknown. Even the familiar jingles that bemuse the children at bed-time are not fully remembered. A glance at the standard texts will show that many are longer in their written forms. Without reason, rhyme dies. Unless it has some other liveliness, like humour, imagination or skill, there is no point in saying it to children, who promptly ask questions that can't be answered. So mothers are doubting the worth of nursery rhymes and turning to other reading-books. If a verse about an animal is wanted, then 'The Cat in the Hat' is better; and if no verse at all is wanted, but only the animal, then books with hideous elephants and toothy rabbits flaunt themselves.

Restoration of reason means re-creation of the poem, which will find its former audience, reborn. Having connected the innocent animals to their adult symbolism, they fit poems of experience. Occasionally, I had to modernize the wording, to convey that experience. The old dress had become a disguise. The work of keeping the poems up to date, which should have been done by generations of folk-poets, had to be done all at once. Additionally, I gave some of them titles, to represent them today.

Restored to their senses, they tell about the suppressed past, the suppressed present. They are all the gossip of the people, condensed and codified. That cultural tradition, from more than one millennium, is not to be ignored because we are now detached from it. New roots are old.

Courtship Rhymes

London Bridge

No. 306, ODNR

London Bridge is broken down,
Broken down, broken down,
London Bridge is broken down,
My fair lady.

Build it up with wood and clay,
Wood and clay, wood and clay,
Build it up with wood and clay,
My fair lady.

All the other verses follow this pattern, so I give their
first lines only.

Wood and clay will wash away . . .
Build it up with bricks and mortar . . .
Bricks and mortar will not stay . . .
Build it up with iron and steel . . .
Iron and steel will bend and bow . . .
Build it up with silver and gold . . .
Silver and gold will be stolen away . . .
Set a man to watch all night . . .
Suppose the man should fall asleep? . . .
Give him a pipe to smoke all night . . .
(c.1825)

OTHER VERSIONS:

'London Bridge' is first recorded, as the title of a
dance, in 1779. The first words are recorded in 1744.
I quote them where they differ significantly from the
modern version:

London Bridge
Is broken down
With a gay lady.

[Last verse]
Then we'll set
A man to watch
With a gay lady.

The version of 1898 offers different ways to keep the man awake:

Suppose the man should fall asleep?
Give him a pipe of tobacco to smoke . . .
Give him a bag of nuts to crack . . .
Give him a horse to gallop around . . .
Set a dog to bark all night . . .
Set a cock to crow all night.
If the cock should meet a hen?
Here comes my lord Duke, let everyone pass by but the very last one.

There is a reference to London Bridge in a play of 1659:
'Thou shalt be the Lady of the Town.'
'I have been one in my days, when we kept the Whitsun Ale, where we danced the building of London Bridge upon wool-packs, and the hay upon a grass-plot, and when we were weary with dancing hard, we always went to the cushion dance.'
There are versions of the rhyme in Germany, Denmark, France, Italy, Hungary, and Scandinavia. One German version is: 'I'd like very much to go over the Magdeburg Bridge.' 'It's broken down.' 'Who broke it down?' 'The goldsmith, the goldsmith, with his youngest daughter . . .'
The French version has: 'The last girl will cross it

three times, three times she'll cross it; and that last girl will stay there.'

Editors have never tried to make sense of nursery rhymes, so they abandon any attempt to punctuate them properly. If the reader will glance through that ODNR printing of London Bridge, he will see many commands and one question. Both indicate that this rhyme is a dialogue; inverted commas, therefore, should have been placed around each verse.

That, in turn, shows that 'my fair lady' is only one of the speakers. There must be another—to try to carry out those commands, to answer that question. Who? Well, who says 'my fair lady'? Probably, a young man. Why would he call her fair? Because he likes her.

We can even get a hint of the whole subject of this rhyme, from this train of thought, from the simple desire to punctuate the rhyme correctly. For, if the young man is speaking to a young lady, and likes her, the chance of their talk being of love is quite high.

However, I am aware that this thinking is assumption. I must not build my bridge on insecure foundations. I will add a support. The title is first known as that of a dance. Who dances?

Our thinking on the main characters must coincide with our thinking on the meaning of the narrative. What does London Bridge being broken down, and being rebuilt, mean? For, it doesn't mean what it says—not with the suggestion that it should be built with silver and gold, not with telling 'my fair lady' all about it.

The meaning should be made clear at the end of the rhyme. But there is no real end to this story at all. We aren't told if the bridge did get rebuilt or not. And we certainly can't understand what the man and his pipe-smoking have got to do with it. That is no conclusion.

So here, at the end, there has been suppression.

Here is the sign of 'bad-joining' I spoke of in the Introduction. There is no join at all! Here is where we must consult the sources and take thought. My thinking is that the rhyme seems to be moving towards a climax, when a correct solution will be made on how to re-build this bridge. I do not think that the bridge can be left 'broken down'. For that would be anti-climax and would not fit the development of the story—the building-materials have been getting more and more precious, have already reached silver and gold, so that it's hard to think of more valuable ones, and yet they aren't considered right. At that juncture, the nursery rhyme suddenly takes the turn of setting a man to watch all night, and keeping him awake—and then stops. Somehow, this man being kept awake has to fit onto the precious building-materials and solve the problem of how to rebuild London Bridge.

What do the sources say? The first printed version, says 'With a gay lady' and, significantly, that it was a gay lady who broke it down in the first place! The version of 1898 links with our current nursery rhyme by including the 'pipe of tobacco to smoke' but then goes onto the 'nuts to crack', the 'dog to bark', the 'horse to gallop around'. What do I make of these? I find that they are all figurative, all sexual symbols. The 'nuts' are still common speech for the testicles (and have the same significance in 'I Had A Little Nut Tree'). The dog is still known as a 'gay dog'. The 'cock' is the best-known phallic symbol we have. And the 'horse', too, still does a good gallop.

And this interpretation all fits the curious dialogue I quote from the play of 1659. The dancing couple, one of whom is the speaker, who has been a Lady of the Town, dances the building (not the falling-down) of London Bridge on wool-packs—and when weary of dancing hard, goes to the cushion dance. What dance can you dance on a wool-pack?

The versions from France and Germany fit my understanding. The German one emphasizes that it was the youngest daughter of the goldsmith who broke the bridge, as the 'gay lady' did. The French version has the girl going across it three times and then 'staying there'. The bridge will not stand more than three times. After that, she is in a different state. How the imagery begins to build up!

I conclude that the bridge is a phallic symbol. These ladies broke it. But 'my fair lady' can rebuild it (at least twice more). And why London Bridge? Because it was the biggest bridge—the longest—in England. Would anyone like to check the grandeur of the Magdeburg Bridge at the appropriate date?

How do I restore my fair lady's successful method, her verse? Now I know the main meaning, I can deduce it.

First, I deduce the form of the rhyme. At the moment, it hasn't got one. The verses are not held together—the two singers would find it difficult to remember their order. Rhyme is the bond of verse. There is just faint sign of it here. 'Wood and clay' do 'wash away'. The other verses have no rhymes. But, looked at critically, I see that 'iron and steel' should 'bend and yield' (not 'bow'); that 'silver and gold' 'away are stoled' (not 'stolen away'). In fact, each verse did once rhyme with the following one. The rhyme scheme, as well as the bridge, broke down.

Now, the last verse has to be 'London Bridge is builded up' to fit the repeated 'Build it up', and to oppose the beginning 'London Bridge is broken down'. So my fair lady's verse has got to rhyme with 'up'.

Of course, my composition of that verse may not be the 'right' one—if it could ever be checked against the lost original. But it must be a possible variant, a version, such as all folk songs have. It has been so

24

guided by the whole length of the rhyme that it cannot be far out. The possible slight error is the price that has to be paid for making sense, for reviving the song.

London Bridge (Restored)

'London Bridge has fallen down,
Fallen down, fallen down,
London Bridge has fallen down,
My fair lady.'

'Build it up with sand and stone,
Sand and stone, sand and stone,
Build it up with sand and stone,
My young laddie.'

'Sand and stone will wash away,
Wash away, wash away,
Sand and stone will wash away,
My fair lady.'

'Build it up with brick and clay,
Brick and clay, brick and clay,
Build it up with brick and clay,
My young laddie.'

'Brick and clay they will not stay,
Will not stay, will not stay,
Brick and clay they will not stay,
My fair lady.'

'Build it up with iron and steel,
Iron and steel, iron and steel,
Build it up with iron and steel,
My young laddie.'

'Iron and steel will bend and yield,
Bend and yield, bend and yield,
Iron and steel will bend and yield
My fair lady.'

'Build it up with silver and gold,
Silver and gold, silver and gold,
Build it up with silver and gold,
My young laddie.'

'Silver and gold away are stoled,
Away are stoled, away are stoled,
Silver and gold away are stoled,
My fair lady.'

'Set a man a watch to keep,
Watch to keep, watch to keep,
Set a man a watch to keep,
My young laddie.'

'Say the man should fall asleep?
Fall asleep, fall asleep,
Say the man should fall asleep?
My fair lady.'

'Let the man lie in my lap,
In my lap, in my lap,
Let the man lie in my lap,
My young laddie.'

'London Bridge is builded up!
Builded up, builded up,
London Bridge is builded up!
My fair lady.'

Upon Paul's Steeple
No. 397, ODNR

Upon Paul's steeple stands a tree
As full of apples as maybe;
The little boys of London town
They run with hooks to pull them down;
And then they go from hedge to hedge
Until they come to London Bridge.
(1846)

OTHER VERSIONS:

Atop of Paul's steeple there did I see
a delicate, dainty, fine apple tree.
The apples were ripe, and ready to fall,
and killed seven hundred men on a stall.
(1676)

As St Paul's lost its steeple in 1561, the rhyme must be much older than even this version.

It was the illumination on the size of London Bridge which lit up Paul's steeple. It was chosen because it was the biggest steeple! On the highest erection known stood this image of the great apple tree whose fruit is sought by lads. When they've got it, they can come to mighty London Bridge.

What is this image of the apple tree? Apples are red. It is when they are 'ripe and ready to fall' that they kill men. This image of red ripeness on top of the tallest steeple makes an addition to the phallic symbol. It's like putting a red top-knot on an Easter Island God. Only symbolically does the fall of these apples kill men. For this fruit is from the Tree of Life—and the apple tree has always been used for a symbol of fertility, even of success. 'Old Roger' has the planting of an apple tree, and the fruit growing ripe, as the reviving force for him.

So the boys run to the tree on the height, gather its fruit and then move onto the further symbol of length and strength, London Bridge.

As I've already taken away some of the poetry from the symbols by my flat explanation, I'll put it back by quoting the song the Durham miners sing about something else red: 'What have I made of me red herring's ribs? Bloody great tower, and bloody great bridge.' The images live on.

Having comprehended the imagery of the song, I felt justified in altering 'from hedge to hedge', though it may well be an original wording. It has no symbolism, and I'm not even sure of its realism. I looked at a map of London in 1500, and there were many gardens shown, but nothing I'd call hedges. But studying the way between St Paul's and London Bridge did give me the symbolism I was seeking— though I may be acting as a folk-poet here, as I warned the reader I would, in the Introduction. Anyone who likes can keep 'hedge to hedge'.

Upon Paul's Steeple (Restored)

Upon Paul's steeple stands a tree
As full of apples as can be;
The lively lads of London Town
They run with hooks to pull them down;
And then they Fleet from Strand to Ditch
Until they Tower by London Bridge!

I Had a Little Nut Tree

No. 381, ODNR

I had a little nut tree,
Nothing would it bear
But a silver nutmeg
And a golden pear;
The King of Spain's daughter
Came to visit me,
And all for the sake
Of my little nut tree.

(1797)

OTHER VERSIONS:

I had a silver nettle tree
(1850)

An additional couplet is recorded:

I skipp'd over water, I danced over sea,
And all the birds in the air couldn't catch me.
(1853)

After the apple tree, here is the nut tree. Both are images of male power. Man's strongest drive has found many outlets in imagery. As one of the sources shows, even the botanically unknown nettle-tree can be used, presumably because nettles sting, or prick.

Although the apple tree image is no longer known in Britian, the nut tree is, in America. A firm that was exporting biscuits there, had to change the name of Ginger Nuts because of its associations. Hence the expression 'Oh nuts!' Even in Britain this meaning is half-known. There is a music-hall song which goes:

I've got a lovely bunch of coconuts;
Every ball you bowl will make me rich,
There stands me wife, the idol of me life,
Singing roll or bowl a ball a penny a pitch.

Surely singer and audience know there is a *double entendre* on balls and coconuts?

This interpretation of the meaning of the nut tree is carried on by its characteristics:

Nothing could it bear
But a silver nutmeg
And a golden pear.

The nutmeg is simply a small nut. The progenitor bears a son. And the pear, by its shape, is a symbol of woman. So the tree can also bear a daughter. Only those two, son and daughter, are the fruit of this tree.

The symbolism of the tree is sustained by:

'The King of Spain's daughter
Came to visit me
And all for the sake of my little nut tree.'

The sense is, 'Even the daughter of the King of Spain, of the greatest king in the world.' ODNR mentions a theory that the visit of Juana of Castile is intended in this rhyme. Surely the limitation of that incident, in time and effect, would have limited the popularity of the rhyme. Only one person would have properly sung it! The 'me' would have to be some English prince. From him to a folk-rhyme? Only if a folk truth is conveyed.

That a man should find something to sing about in his attractive power, yes, that does seem a popular subject. All the men in Britain will sing 'me' to that.

The couplet I quote from 1853 suggests that there

was another verse. If the 'skipped over water, danced over sea' is the journey of the King of Spain's daughter (and not of 'me', which, in my interpretation, must be a mistake), then there is the basis for one. Only the basis, because 'water' and 'sea' are repetition, and 'mountain' and 'sea' fit far better.

That new verse, in its turn, suggests that further re-creation is needed, to keep the balance of the song. So I composed a further four-line verse, using the same imagery. Purists, if that is the right word for them, can easily take it out again, if they must have factual, textual support. I wrote it to make the song better, so it would be sung more.

I Had a Little Nut Tree (Restored)

I had a little nut tree
Nothing would it bear
But a silver nut meg
And a golden pear.

The King of Spain's daughter
She came to visit me
And all for the sake
Of my little nut tree.

She took it to her garden
And planted it right there,
It fruited like a fountain
With nut and golden pear.

She came over mountain,
She came over sea,
And all for the sake
Of my little nut tree.

Where Have All the Young Men Gone?

No. 150, ODNR

Eeny, weeny, winey, wo,
Where do all the Frenchmen go?
To the east and to the west,
And into the old crow's nest.

(1883?)

OTHER VERSIONS:

Eana, meena, mina, mo,
Where do all the Frenchmen go?
To the east, to the west,
To the bonny bird's nest;
Apples in the garden,
Fishes in the sea,
If you want a pretty girl,
Please choose me!

(1924)

Hickery, pickery, pease scon,
Where will this young man gang?

(1820)

Iram, biram, brendom, bo,
Where do the sailors go?

(1883)

Eendy, beendy, baniba, roe . . .
(A version of 'Eeena, meena, mina, mo', 1888)

There must be a counterpart to 'I had a little nut-tree'.
And here it is. Women sing their charm, too.
Frenchmen, sailors, young men will all come 'over

mountain, over sea', or 'to the east and to the west', for 'the bonny bird's nest'.

I don't think I have to explain that image. But I'd like to explain its origin. Once, the birds that symbolized man and woman were the robin and the wren. That is why they are still regarded with particular liking today. The wren builds a small, round nest with an entrance hole. So Jenny Wren and her nest become the first symbol of woman. Later, other 'birds' became women!

It is obvious, really, because the first four lines of the second version quoted have to fit onto the plain invitation 'If you want a pretty girl, Please choose me.'

The crow is not a wren. The sailors go to her, and the notorious Frenchmen.

But there has been some bad joining in these versions—always a sign of alteration, deliberate or accidental. The second version should not begin with the Frenchmen, for the girl is seeking a young Englishman for a mate. It will be such a young man, who is seeking the 'bonny bird's nest', and he is mentioned in the third version quoted.

He is invoked with 'Hickery, pickery'-hickery, dickery. For 'hick' was a sixteenth century form of Dick. 'Dick, Dick, peas and corn'—'Dick', and seed.

All the first lines are similarly suggestive. They echo their original calls.

And if the young men are restored to their seeking of some bonny bird, the sailors to the crow, and the first lines made to lead into their different quests, I find that there are two similar rhymes here, not one.

Where Have All the Young Men Gone? (Restored)

Hickery-dickery, peas and corn,
Where do all the young men run?
Some run east, and some run west,
They all run into the blackbird's nest.
Apples in the garden,
Fishes in the sea,
If you want a pretty girl,
Please choose me!

And All the Sailors?

Endy-bendy, winey, rum,
Where do all the sailors come?
Some come east, and some come west,
They all come into the old crow's nest.

OTHER VERSIONS:

Endy-bendy, banana, bo!
Where do all the sailors go?

(restored from the 1888 version); and from the 1883 one:

Hire'em, buy'em, bend'em, bo!

There Was A Pretty Maid . . .
No. 314, ODNR

There was a little maid, and she was afraid
That her sweetheart would come unto her;
So she went to bed, and covered up her head,
And fastened the door with a skewer.

(1844)

There can't be any clearer example of 'little' meaning 'big'. This little girl has a sweetheart. One who could come up to bed. So, if she is 'little', all the other 'little' boys and girls of rhyme may also be old enough.

She isn't really afraid, either. Bed's not a very good place to go, if you're frightened of being slept with.

When she's undressed, she fastens the door with a skewer. That's odd. If she were afraid, she'd fasten it with an iron bar. Then nothing would happen.

So, if she isn't afraid, what does she fasten it with? A skewer is neither thin nor thick. Nor does it rhyme with 'unto her'. Someone put it in to ob-skewer the meaning. What meaning? If she is not afraid, she'd fasten the door with something very slender. Not nothing at all. You can't fasten a door with nothing at all. But with something—just a token.

Then, we'll have a folk-joke, a memorable little rhyme. The restoration is to refind the fun.

There Was a Pretty Maid...
or
A Splintering Crash (Restored)

There was a pretty maid, and she was afraid
That her sweetheart would come into her.
So she went up to bed, put the clothes over her head,
And fastened the door with a splinter!

Bo-Peep
No. 66, ODNR

Little Bo-peep has lost her sheep,
And can't tell where to find them;
Leave them alone, and they'll come home,
And bring their tails behind them.

Little Bo-peep fell fast asleep,
And dreamt she heard them bleating;
But when she awoke, she found it joke,
For they were still all fleeting.

Then up she took her little crook,
Determined for to find them;
She found them indeed, but it made her heart
    bleed,
For they'd left their tails behind them.

It happened one day, as Bo-peep did stray
Into a meadow hard by,
There she espied their tails side by side,
All hung on a tree to dry.

She heaved a sigh, and wiped her eye,
And over the hillocks went rambling,
And tried what she could, as a shepherdess should,
To tack again each to its lambkin.

(1842)

OTHER VERSIONS:

The first verse only was printed in 1805. In 1810 the
song was printed as above, except that the last verse
had 'over the hillocks went stump-o . . . tack each
again to its rump-o.'

36

An Elizabethan ballad has:

Halfe England ys nowght now but shepe,
In everye corner thay playe boe-pepe;

Most people know the first verse only. Once they see
the whole song printed, they do begin to suspect its
double meaning. For lambs can't literally drop tails
like handkerchiefs. And some of the symbols are still
used. We still say, 'She's her mother's pet lamb. Let
her beware of the wolf.' I saw some lads hang a foxtail
on the aerial of their sports-car. They didn't mean they
were hunting foxes. In 'The Ball of Kirremuir', a
modern ballad which some may know, 'hung on a tree
to dry' were 'four and twenty maidenheads'. Just like
these two tails were. 'Remember Tam o'Shanter's
mare.'

For these lambs have been out all night, or very late
at night. Bo-peep had gone to sleep, and dreamt, and
still they hadn't come home. They did return, belatedly;
and their tails were in a meadow, nearby. The wolves
had brought them nearly home.

The mother's heart bleeds, because the lambs' tails
are gone. She will try 'to tack each again to its
lambkin'. Oh, joke at the foolishness of a fond mother!
Mothers do (did?) know that they may have to sigh and
wipe their eye when they have daughters who stay out
very late. And may have to pretend they are still virgin.

Once again, this nursery rhyme shows that 'little'
does not mean 'very young'. This 'little' mother has a
meaningful name. We still use 'peep-bo' for the game
with babies, but it once meant adult putting-out and
withdrawing, as the Elizabethan ballad in the 'Other
Versions' shows. I suspect that professors think it is a
reference to the growth of sheep-farming in England.
'The Chancellor of the Exchequer sits on a 'wool-sack'
etc. But sheep can't play peep-bo. Those sheep, in

modern slang, were cows; and were playing the grande, olde, gayme!

Having understood, I could correct the errors of the 1810 version. The printer of 1805 had played safe by giving only one verse. What would have been thought of anyone who had tried to compose the missing verses if that had been the only edition to survive? I modernized the second verse. 'Bleating' and 'fleating' were correct but are not now. I struggled with 'over the hillocks went rambling' (or 'went stump-o'). If anyone prefers that to my version, please . . . It might be the original line. But it might not, for it does not connect the line before, the 'wiped her eye', with the line after, the 'tried what she could, as a shepherdess should'. So I restored—or composed—an original one.

Bo-Peep
(Restored)

Dame Bo-peep had lost her sheep
And couldn't tell where to find them;
She'd left them alone and thought they'd come home
Bringing their tails behind them.

One night Bo-peep fell fast asleep
And dreamt she heard them Maa-ing;
But when she awoke she was mistook
For they were still ta-taaing.

Then up she took her careful crook
Determined for to find them;
She found them indeed but it made her heart bleed
For they'd left their tails behind them.

It happened next day when she did stray
Into a meadow, sighing,
That there she espied two tails side by side
Hung on a tree a-drying.

She began to cry but wiped her eye
And yet her ill-luck was rankling;
She'd try what she could as a shepherdess should
To tack each on again to its lambkin!

Humpty-Dumpty
No. 233, ODNR

Humpty Dumpty sat on a wall,
Humpty Dumpty had a great fall.
All the king's horses,
And all the king's men,
Couldn't put Humpty together again.
(1830)

OTHER VERSIONS:

Rowly bowly sat on a wall
(1835)

Forty doctors and forty wrights
Couldn't put Humpty Dumpty to rights!
(1846)

This is a rhyme with relatives in France, Sweden, Denmark, Finland, Switzerland and Germany. Relevant portions of some of them are: 'Not all the men in our land/ Can cure Lille Trille' and, 'No doctor in the whole world/Thille Lille can heal' (both from Denmark). 'There is no doctor in the whole land/ Who can help Wirgele-Wargele' and 'There is no doctor in England/Who can cure Humpelken Pumpelken' (both from Germany).

The usual illustration to the rhyme is a broken egg. But why should anyone think it's about eggs? Horses never could put eggs together. The *Oxford English Dictionary* gives the first use of 'Humpty dumpty' in 1785: 'a little humpty dumpty man or woman; a short clumsy person of either sex'.

Is not the name more suggestive of a person than of

an egg? Names given in the other versions are Rowly-Bowly, Wirgele-Wargele and Gigele-Gagele (German), Boule-Boule (French), Annebadadeli (Swiss). So from all over Europe come names suggesting a Rolly-Polly, Wiggly-Waggley, Giggley-Gaggley, Bouncing-Bowly, Diddly-Daddly—girl.

Would all the peoples of Europe have been concerned about a broken hen's egg? Has not 'fall' a very pregnant meaning? A 'great' fall sounds like that—and a small one would have been enough for the egg. I think they were concerned about their daughters' virginity.

This understanding of the rhyme is confirmed by the description of a game, played by girls, which can accompany the saying of it. 'The players sit down holding their skirts tightly about their feet. At an agreed signal, they throw themselves backwards, and must recover their balance without letting go their skirts' (ODNR). These are the eggs that sit on walls, and must take care not to get cracked. If they do, the third English version and several of the foreign ones say that there is no doctor that can help them. Surely that is significant? Doctors never helped eggs.

My difficulty is now poetic. If I restore the original, it is:

Plumpty-Dumpty sat on a wall,
Plumpty-Dumpty had a great fall.
All the king's doctors, all the king's men,
Couldn't put Plumpty together again.

That is no longer meaningful, because we don't use 'put together' in that sense of restoring virginity. It no longer fits a 'fallen' girl. So the rhyme would still not live—the egg would be on the shelf! So I took the liberty, or the duty, of being a folk-poet.

Humpty-Dumpty alias Plumpty-Dumpty (Restored)

Plumpty-Dumpty sat on a wall,
Plumpty-Dumpty had a great fall.
All the king's doctors, all the king's laws,
Couldn't put Plumpty back as she was,
Back as she was, back as she was,
Couldn't put Plumpty back as she was.

Little Miss Muffet
No. 369, ODNR

Little Miss Muffet
Sat on a tuffet,
Eating her curds and whey;
There came a big spider,
Who sat down beside her
And frightened Miss Muffet away.
                    (1805)

OTHER VERSIONS:

Little Mary Ester
Sat upon a tester
          (1812)

Little Miss Mopsey
Sat in the shopsey
          (1842)

The rhyme is pointless. It does not end in wisdom, as Robert Frost might say. Why should people keep repeating such an insignificant story? What can even a child learn from it?

It's an unreasonable rhyme. Why did that spider come? Why did it stop and sit down? Why, come to that, should Miss Muffet be frightened of it, if she were the kind of girl who would take her curds and whey out to a grassy hillock? It's all coincidence, the only meaning it carried: 'Be frightened of spiders'.

Let us use adult vision, instead of a childish blank stare. We need not accept 'little' at nursery value. The love-birds are both little, in 'Two Little Love-birds'. Little Bo-peep is a mother, and Little Dicky Delver is married. 'Little' is a little derogatory, or familiar. Miss Muffet need not be too young.

Then, there is significance in her name. This is Miss Muff-et. If the reader has ever seen a muff, he'll know why it is a female sexual symbol. Another version of the Rhyme calls her Miss Mop-sey. There's a symbolic name made by exactly the same word-formation.

Now, what does she sit on? The 'grassy hillock' is the probable meaning, according to ODNR. There is another dictionary meaning, 'a three-legged stool'. But both those are single meanings, which lead to a single-vision rhyme, without general, symbolic meaning—which the rhyme must have had, to have lived. I think this is 'on her tuff-et'. Scholars have been looking up the wrong word. 'Tuffe' in Chambers' *Twentieth Century Dictionary* is the same as 'tuft' and is a Shakespearean word, as well. So I think this Miss Muff-et was sitting on her (little) tuft. What a different beginning!

Now, this girl is doing something very like 'eating her curds and whey'. Only it's 'heating her curds and way'. 'Way' is given in Partridge's *Dictionary of Slang* as meaning the female part. 'Curds' is not recorded there. But, as they are famous for whiteness, I think 'curds' was known, among the folk, as an image of breasts.

The other versions show that we have not ventured too far in our search for the original meaning. The 'tester' that Mary Ester sits on must surely be a bed? The word can mean either a sixpence or a piece of head-armour or a bed-canopy. Of those three, I think only the bed-canopy is possible. Little Miss Mopsey, who sat in the shop-sey, must have had some reason for sitting there. She must have been on display, or even on sale. In all three cases, the nursery cannot explain why they should sit there, eating a sort of yoghurt. But these are the places where a young miss might sit. And not with legs crossed, as mother taught.

Now, we have to follow this very different beginning by taking hints from the nursery rhyme. Obviously, it's no big spider who comes to such a girl. But 'spider' is near, in sound, to 'spied her'. And, if Miss Muff-et, Miss Mop-sey and Mary Ester are 'heating their curds and way', someone will, indeed, spy them. And come and sit down beside them. A man.

So, the two halves of the rhyme are beginning to join, to be reasonable. There's cause and effect.

The rhyme should end in folk-wisdom, a teaching about life, as so many folk-songs do. The end of this one was simply that Miss Muffet was frightened away. That is not strong enough to be the true ending—it's nearly anti-climax. This girl has broken the conventions, along has come a man, who saw her, and then—what?

I had noticed that 'tuft' on which Miss Muff-et sat, was also a verb, meaning 'to separate into tufts; to beat, as a covert'. This man who spied her and sat down beside her might 'beat her, as a covert' or separate her muff into tufts. She would be a warning to others.

Little Miss Muffet (Restored)

Little Miss Muffet
Sat on her tuffet
Heating her curds and way;
There came one who spied her,
And sat down beside her,
And tufted her muffet away.

To the Withdrawn Snail
No. 482 ODNR

Snail, snail,
Come out of your hole,
Or else I'll beat you
As black as coal.

Snail, snail,
Put out your horns,
I'll give you bread
And barley corns.
(1744)

OTHER VERSIONS:

Buckie, buckie snail, cock out your horn,
And I'll give you bread and butter the morn.
(1901)

Shell a muddy, shell a muddy,
Put out your horns,
For the king's daughter is coming to town
With a red petticoat and a green gown.

There are versions of the rhyme from all over the world.
From France:—'Colimacon borgne,
Montre-moi tes cornes' etc. (Snail the one-eyed,
Show me your horns).
From Russia:—'Snail, snail, put forth thy horns,
I will give thee cakes.'
From Spain:—'Snail, snail, put out your horns to the sun,
So that your father and mother also put them out.'
From China:—'Snail, snail, come here to be fed,

Put out your horns and lift up your head,
Father and mother will give you to eat,
Good boiled mutton shall be your meat.'

Finally, there is another English Nursery Rhyme, which includes snails:
What are little boys made of?
Snakes, and snails, and puppy-dogs' tails . . .

The two verses of the rhyme cannot be the complete version, because they do not conclude. So my task is to draw the snail on, out of his shell.

From the other sources quoted comes the knowledge of how to charm him. All of them show the snail as a phallic symbol,—men, the world over, threatening or bribing it to put out its horn(s). The Scotch version is very clear, with its 'cock-out'. And the Irish, describing the girl's provocative petticoat and gown the colour of grass when she comes to meet him, is also an illustration of his meaning. Is she the King of Spain's daughter? The French one interested me, because of its description of the snail. No natural snail was ever called 'one-eyed'. Yet that's a vivid adjective for the 'winkle', as some Englishmen still call it.

The Spanish invocation I read a lot into. First, that the phallic power should be shown to the sun, as that was the supreme pagan god; second, that the male power linked the bearer with his father and mother— with his ancestors. There is no necessity for this interpretation in the English rhyme—but I find it intensely interesting. See how the Chinese—still renowned for reverencing their ancestors—also say 'Father and mother will give you to eat.' I recall how intent the Chinese are—or have been—on retaining potency, how they pay immense sums for rhinoceros horn. It has a harder horn than a snail!

What these many versions show is that snails live all over the world, that men have observed their stretching forward and have linked it with their own bodies and desires.

So we have the subject matter certainly. But how to proceed with the verses? The foreign sources help us, and real life. The snail is not completely out when it puts out its horns. If I remember, or observe, what next it does, I shall see how the invocation must proceed. The foreign sources help by suggesting other foods as further rewards ('cakes' from Russia; 'bread and butter' from the other English version; 'boiled mutton' all the way from China.) Obviously, any food, ordinary or rare, which fits the 'cock out your horn'. So, a version can be composed which can only be on the right lines; can only be one of many possible versions. But do not dismiss the live snail because its tail is my graft, or he will die in your mind, where his living is important, as it has been for hundreds of years. 'So that your father and mother also put them out.'

To the Withdrawn Snail (Restored)

Snail, snail,
Come out of your hole,
Or else I'll beat you
As black as coal.

Snail, snail,
Put out your horns.
I'll give you bread
And barley-corns.

Snail, snail,
Put out your neck.
I'll give you well-hung
Hare to peck.

Snail, snail,
Raise up your head.
I'll give you a cushion,
For your bed.

Snail, snail,
Lay out your track.
I'll give you my life-blood
Not to go back.

Jack and Jill
No. 254, ODNR

Jack and Jill went up the hill,
To fetch a pail of water;
Jack fell down and broke his crown,
And Jill came tumbling after.
(1765)

Up Jack got, and home did trot,
As fast as he could caper,
To old Dame Dob, who patched his nob
With vinegar and brown paper.
    (This second verse added in *c.* 1800)

Then Jill came in,
And she did grin,
To see Jack's paper plaster;
Her mother whipt her,
Across her knee,
For laughing at Jack's disaster.
(1820)

OTHER VERSIONS:

The illustration to the first printing (1765) shows two boys.

Jack and Jill were the known names of the typical courting pair. 'Jack shall have Jill; Nought shall go ill; The man shall have his mare again; And all shall be well.' That's from *A Midsummer Night's Dream,* where much pairing takes place. Incidentally, what's the meaning of 'mare' in the quotation?

So that disposes of little boy and little girl. Now, 'up' the hill to get water! That's as peculiar a direction as the season is in 'Here we come gathering nuts in May.' Our young couples go into woods to gather bluebells—they're more realistic in their excuse.

Then one falls down and breaks his (or her) crown. I have to begin my changes here. For there have been sex changes made in this rhyme, in order to hide the meaning. In 1765, even in the broad-minded eighteenth century, the rhyme was being disguised. That first printing tried to mislead by showing the pair as two boys. Why make that sex-change, unless the original rhyme was sexual?

I think it was Jill who fell down and broke her crown, and Jack who came tumbling after. 'Tumbling' has a second meaning. 'Crown', too, must have sexual meaning, for a bride wears one. It must signify, in her case, virginity. If it carries that sense here, it would make sense of the original falling down, and the haste with which the second person follows the first. Let us not forget that this pair did not go up the hill to fetch a pail of water.

On to the second verse. Dame Dob can be dismissed because Jack is not a little boy. The form of the line—'To old Dame Dob, who patched his nob'—confirms our rejection, because it has eight syllables when it should have seven. With her go the remedies. For my understanding of breaking a crown is not so 'little'. But the beginning of the verse is near the original. When the girl has lain down, Jack would get up and do something or other as fast as he could.

If the 'vinegar and brown paper' are literal patchings to hide the real falling-down, and Jack's quick response, what are they replacing? Here, form helps—it is, indeed, all there is to guide us. Form insists that this second pair of lines should be about Jill, to balance the first pair about Jack. From the beginning, the verse has told of them both. So, if the second verse begins with Jack doing something as fast as he can, it should end with Jill doing something as 'slowly' as she can. Her lines should contrast.

The third verse I have no use for. It is obviously badly formed—even the internal rhyme the third line needs, has been omitted. Also, the content is so Victorian, so moral and—again—so babyish. Someone has, very crudely, composed a third verse to follow the incidents in the second. That someone has done the opposite of restoration—his 'tail' is unnecessary and destroys the original meaning of the courting pair's story

Jack and Jill (Restored)

Jack and Jill went up the hill
To fetch a pail of water;
Jill fell down, and cracked her crown,
And Jack came tumbling after.

Then up Jack got and on did trot
As fast as he could court her;
Jill lay still—her pail* did fill
With milk and not with water.

'Pail' is slang for vagina—Partridge's *Dictionary of Slang*.

Coming Through the Rye
No. 253, ODNR

Jack and Gye
Went out in the rye,
And they found a little boy with one black eye.
Come, says Jack, let's knock him on the head.
No, says Gye, let's buy him some bread;
You buy one loaf and I'll buy two,
And we'll bring him up as other folk do.

(c. 1850)

I am aware that my interpretation, and restoration, of 'Jack and Jill' may need a little strengthening. It's a shock for most people. So I add this almost unknown rhyme, to show the kind of tale folk did repeat.

This starts much the same. The young couple go out in the rye —are they picking bluebells?—and find 'a little boy with one black eye'. Now the sort of innocence that takes that literally is too like ignorance for me. The little 'one eyed' boy must be a description of the phallus. Jack could not literally have suggested killing a little boy—surely?

What Jill wants is 'to bring him up'—by something they can do in the rye. Not going back to the village baker and buying bread—in such odd numbers of loaves—but by behaving as other courting couples do.

Coming Through the Rye (Restored)

Jack and Jill went out in the rye
And found a little boy with only one eye.
'Oh' says Jack 'I think he's dead.'
'No' says Gye 'Let's give him some bread.
You give him one roll and I'll give him two.
And we'll bring him up like other folk do.'

Baa, Baa, Black Sheep

No. 55, ODNR

Baa, Baa, black sheep,
Have you any wool?
Yes, sir, yes, sir,
Three bags full;
One for the master,
And one for the dame,
And one for the little boy
Who lives down the lane.
(1843?)

OTHER VERSIONS:

Bah, Bah, a black sheep,
Have you any wool,
Yes merry have I,
Three bags full,
One for my master,
One for my dame,
One for my little boy
That lives in the lane.
(1744)

There are two speakers, this 'sir' and the black sheep.
Sir begins, black sheep replies. There ought to be
inverted commas round each of their speeches to give
realism . . .

But it's not a very real question to ask a sheep if it's
got any wool. It'd be a funny sheep without any. This
one has a lot. A wool-pack, if that's what she means,
weighs 240 lbs. She gives the three bags not to the
farmer and his wife only: one goes to the little boy
down the lane. The farmer won't be pleased. Do
sheep, real sheep, give their wool to who ever they

like? Do real sheep talk to gentlemen?

If it isn't a real sheep, it's someone in sheep's clothing. This is a girl, or a woman, because a sheep is not a ram. Sheep have been used before, in 'Bo-peep', to mean girls. This one is more than just a girl: she's a bad girl. She's a black sheep, and there's only one way in folk-thinking for a girl to be bad. Black is the opposite of white, the colour of virginity. So, black is sexual love. Hence the Black Bull Inn. 'She's the black sheep of the family,' people would say.

We now have a meaningful start. 'Baa, Baa, miss black sheep, have you any wool?' 'Yes sir, yes sir, three bags full.' What a strong reply! Two yeses, three bags and all full. She's got some wool all right.

The second version even has 'Baa' spelt 'Bah' as if the gentleman were being scornful of her. And then, 'Yes, merry have I'. What's merry about having three bales of ordinary wool?

This black sheep isn't talking about ordinary wool. She's talking about how much loving she's got. The wool is her curly hair. She's sure she's got a lot of it to give merrily away.

Then everyone who gets it will be a man! So 'dame' is an alteration. We can see proof of that in the word itself. For 'dame' is not the true opposite of 'master'. 'Mistress' is. But 'master' and 'man' are the true opposites, once we see she doesn't care about the social standing of her men.

The 'little boy' can get a bag-full of her wool, provided we realize—from the previous rhymes—that 'little' doesn't mean too young. It just means someone she's familiar with. He's called 'my' little boy, originally. Now, a daftly-real sheep might senti-mentally say 'my master' and 'my dame', but not 'my little boy'. Even daftly-real sheep in sentimental rhymes don't have boy children.

So 'my little boy' means my favourite young man. Why would he be her favourite? Because he's a young Black Bull.

Baa, Baa, Black Sheep (Restored)

'Baa, Baa, black sheep,
Have you any wool?'
'Yes sir, yes sir,
Three bags full!
One for the master,
And one for the man,
And one for the little lad
Who tups like a ram!'

A Ring, A Ring O' Roses
No. 443, ODNR

Ring-a-ring o' roses,
A pocket full of posies,
A-tishoo! A-tishoo!
We all fall down.

     (1898)

OTHER VERSIONS:

A ring, a ring o' roses,
A pocketful of posies,
Ash-a! Ash-a!
All stand still.

The King has sent his daughter
To fetch a pail of water,
Ash-a! Ash-a!
All bow down.

The bird above the steeple
Sits high above the people,
Ash-a! Ash-a!
All kneel down.

The wedding bells are ringing
And boys and girls are singing,
Ash-a! Ash-a!
All fall down.

     (1915)

A curtsey here, a curtsey there,
A curtsey to the ground, sir.

     (1882)

There are German, French and Gaelic versions.

The German is: 'Ring a ring a row. The children are three. They sit on the elder-bush. They all shout 'Musch, musch, musch'. Sit down! The wife sits in the ring, with seven little children. What do they like to eat? Little fish. What do they like to drink? Red wine. Sit down!'

The French is: 'Dance, roll, daughter of Alexander. The peach is ripe, the fig is very ripe, the rose-bush all in flower. Cuckoo! Trollop! Clap! Clap hands. The cow is in the garden. Down ye go! Down ye go! Get up now, get up! Let's do it again.'

There is also an English sequel, to get the dancers to their feet:

The cows are in the garden,
Lying fast asleep.
A-tishoo! A-tishoo!
We all get up again.

There is a modern parody.

Ring-a-ring o' geranium,
A pocketful o' uranium,
Hi-roshima,
All fall down!

(1949)

This will be the restoration of happiness, for the rhyme we know is supposed to refer to the Black Death. But the folk-song, we don't know, refers to wedding bells. It's those I want to hear ring again. Happiness is good for us, but unhappiness is a sort of Black Death, only good if you develop an immunity to it.

Let's develop an immunity to this Black Death explanation. Let's throw it off like the plague. It declares that a rosy rash was a sign of disease, that a posy of herbs was a protection against it, that sneezing was the last symptom before falling down dead.

A ring of roses is not a rosy rash. Would any mother call the rash on her baby's bottom a ring of roses? She would not, because the rash might be circular but would not be a ring. And 'roses' is too nice a word for a nasty rash.

'A pocketful of posies'. Who said the posy was a bunch of herbs? Normally, it's a bunch of flowers. Then, how many bunches are wanted? Why isn't one enough?

The 'A-tishoo! A-tishoo!' is in only two of the twelve versions collected before 1898. Only after that did it become accepted. The other ten versions show that the fall was not a fall, but a 'curtsy or other gracious bending movement' (ODNR). No song about the Black Death ever ended with a curtsy.

'Don't think what you want to think before you know what you ought to know.' I looked up bubonic plague in Black's *Medical Dictionary*. 'Fever, headache, lassitude . . . features drawn, eyes sunken, stupor and wild delirium.' No mention of sneezing. 'Swollen glands in groins, or armpits.' Those are the buboes. 'The haemorrages under the skin make black, gangrenous patches.' Black patches! Of course! It's the Black Death. But no rosy ones.

Am I the first to refer to a medical book? The ODNR says, 'A rosy rash, they allege, was a symptom of the plague.' They allege. Is that cover? Did the editors know what they ought to have known and covered it up? 'It would be more delightful to recall the old belief that gifted children had the power to laugh roses.' Ought I to know that? Or am I being mythified?

We accepted the Black Death explanation because we live under the threat of war. It suits us. We are throwing our own black, deathly fear over the song.

We have made the 'Hiro-shima, All fall down' parody, and quoted it. The title, 'The Dance of Death', has been imprinted in our minds.

The French, German, and Gaelic versions aren't full of death. They're full of love and life. The German wife has seven children, eating and drinking fish and wine. The French girls rocks and rolls. The Gaelic song wants the dancers to get up and do it again. And so does our English sequel. Do what again?

The song of 1915 shows the meaning. It's the words of a ring-dance. There are two rings. The first is the ring of girls. And they are called, poetically, roses. Is that too poetic? Then what about the 'rose-bush all in flower' of the French version? The lads form the second ring. They are the 'pocketful of posies'—or words similar to those. These are lads, wanting to get married. What have they got pocketfuls of, that might resemble 'posies'?

The first verse ends 'All stand still'. That fits a ring-dance. It doesn't have the 'All fall down' until the last verse, until after 'The wedding bells are ringing/The boys and girls are singing'—until, in other words, it can't possibly mean 'All fall down dead.'

By taking the 'All fall down', the rhyme shows it has come from the folk-song. It couldn't have been taken, and misplaced, if it weren't there to take! So the folk-song is earlier than the rhyme, even though it was collected later. IT is the original.

This dance is a wedding-dance. So the 'pail of water', in verse two, is what every girl gets when she's a rose ready to open. The water is a sort of sap. The bird that sits high above the people, on the steeple, in verse three, is the cock. He'd better come too. He may be needed. He crows for a little sun and air! The folk jokes begin to fit the folk-songs!

All we're left to make sense of is that 'Ash-a! Ash-a!' of the folk-song, the 'A-tishoo!' of the rhyme.

It's meaningless because it's only a part. It's the part of the words you'd hear as the young men and women danced as they sang. The exclamation marks give the first clue. The 'a!' is exclaimed, emphasized, and sounds 'ya', like the 'yoo' sound at the end of A-tishyoo. Both 'ya' and 'yoo' are the same sound as 'you'. 'Ash-you' or 'ish-you' were the endings of the words.

Just before the boys and girls made that gracious bending movement, they sang some words that ended with 'ash-you' or 'ish-you'. Just before the wedding bells, they sang those same words. Before wedding, comes courting. Before 'issue' comes 'kiss you'.

If people can solve crosswords, they can solve happy-words! Then we can all kiss, lie down and stand up again. For the folk-song is no longer a puzzel.

A Ring, A Ring O'Roses (Restored)

A ring, a ring o' roses,
A pocketful o' nosegays,
I kiss you, I kiss you,
We all stand still.

The cock upon the steeple
Stands high above the people,
I kiss you, I kiss you,
We all bow down.

The queen has sent her daughter
To fetch a pail of water,
I kiss you, I kiss you,
We all kneel down.

The wedding bells are ringing,
The boys and girls are singing,
I kiss you, I kiss you,
We all lie down.

The English Sequel to
A Ring, A Ring O'Roses

The cow has left the garden,
The horn has lost its harden,
I kiss you, I kiss you,
We all stand up.

Marriage Rhymes

Little Dicky Delve-and-Dig 'er
No. 133, ODNR

Little Dicky Dilver
Had a wife of silver;
He took a stick and broke her back
And sold her to the miller;
The miller wouldn't have her
So he threw her in the river.

(1844)

OTHER VERSIONS:

Little Dicky Diller
Had a wife of siller;
He took a stick and broke her back,
And sent her to the miller.

The miller with his stone dish
Sent her unto Uncle Fish.

Uncle Fish, the good shoemaker,
Sent her unto John the baker.

John the baker, with his ten men,
Sent her unto Mistress Wren.

Mistress Wren, with grief and pain,
Sent her to the Queen of Spain.

The Queen of Spain, that woman of sin,
Opened the door and let her in.

(c. 1900)

The Other Version is the ribs and backbone of Little Dicky, and the nursery rhyme is the skull that's rolled away from them, kicked and broken.

As always, and for ever, let us make the dry bones live.

First, let us set the backbone straight. Dicky Delver has a wife. She is sent to the miller, the shoemaker, the baker and then on to Mistress Wren and the Queen of Spain.

Those people had reputations. The miller was known for grinding seed. The shoemaker threw shoes at weddings. John the baker put buns in the oven. Mistress Wren was well-known for having many children. She was like the Old Woman who lived in a shoe. A rhyme about her goes:

The dove says 'Coo, Coo, what shall I do?
I can scarce maintain two.'
'Pooh, pooh,' says the wren 'I have ten
And keep them all like gentlemen.'

From her, with her brood, the wife goes to visit the Queen of Spain. We are told what she is famous for. Sin. What sin can it be that followed from having many children?

Was even a wife thought sinful in 1900 if she had a lot of children? Yes, if she spoke happily about making them. The proper attitude was that sex and mother-hood were a duty, a sacrifice. 'In sorrow shalt thou bring forth children,' Genesis 4:16.

But Mistress Wren is too old a bird to be caught with chaff like that. She's from pagan times, when she was a sacred woman-symbol. Grief, pain, and sexual sin belong to that new-comer, Eve.

The Queen of Spain is a late substitute for the Great One, the Queen of Women, who opens the door and takes them in when they're pregnant.

For there is the backbone of the story—the journey of the wife through sex and pregnancy to motherhood. We can attach the disjointed parts to it. 'Wife of silver' is just an attempt to make a rhyme with Dilver. But that name itself is a mistake. Dicky Delver is his name, because he digs and delves his wife's fertile earth.

'Broke her back' is just the opposite attempt—an attempt to avoid the rhyme that made the sense. It should be 'He took a stick and thrashed her *rick*', because that leads on to sending her to the miller. The miller can deal with a wife whose rick has been thrashed, but not with one who has a broken back.

'A stone dish' is not the sign of a miller. He has stones, certainly, for his grinding. The flour will go straight to John the baker.

His 'ten men' are an echo of the sound of his 'oven', plus a memory of the ten that Mistress Wren had.

Now little Dicky is put together again. What he needs is just a touch of life, to make him flesh and blood. His wife must become quick-silver! And he, he needs his full, double-barrelled surname. When I found those, them bones, them bones, them dry bones, they heard the name of the Lord!

Little Dicky Delve-and-Dig'er (Restored)

Little Dicky Delve-and-Dig'er
Had a wife he would make bigger.

He took a stick and thrashed her rick
And sent her on to Miller Dick.

Miller Dick, with grinding stones,
Sent her on to Baker Jones.

Baker Jones, with big round oven,
Sent her on to Mistress Wren.

Mistress Wren, with kindly mirth,
Sent her on to Mother Earth.

Mother Earth, with welcome good,
Sent her on to motherhood.

How Many Miles to Babylon?
No. 26, ODNR

How many miles to Babylon?
Three score miles and ten.
Can I get there by candle-light?
Yes, and back again.
If your heels are nimble and light,
You may get there by candle-light.
(1894?)

OTHER VERSIONS:

King and Queen of Cantylon,
How many miles to Babylon?
Eight and eight, and other eight.
Will I get there by candle-light?
If your horse be good and your spurs be bright.
How many men have ye?
Mae nor ye *daur* come and see.   [more;dare]
(1824?)

Fox a fox, a brummalary,
How many miles to Lummaflary?
Lummabary. Eight and eight, and a
   hundred and eight.
How shall I get home tonight?
Spin your legs and run fast.
(1853)

Chick my *naggie,* chick my *naggie!*   [From 'nag']
How many miles to Aberdeagie?
'Tis eight, and eight, and other eight.
We'll no win there wi' candle-light.
(1801)

The King and Queen of Cantylon know how far it is to Babylon. Their kingdom and Babylon must be in touch. Where are these places?

First, they are both lands. That 'lon' is a mis-hearing, or mis-spelling, of 'land'. The King and Queen of Cantyland are asked how far it is to Babbyland. That spelling is old-fashioned, because the old way of saying baby was babby. I've heard my grandmother use it. So Cantyland is in touch with Babyland.

This Cantyland is called Lummaflary in one of the Other Versions. 'Lum' means chimney. So Lummaflary is the place where the chimney's on fire. Can we now call Cantyland, Cuntyland? It is the place where the chimney's on fire, and bare; and it needs a king and queen to rule it. 'King and Queen of Cuntyland, How far is it to Babyland?'

That is the question. It's as important as 'To be, or not to be.'

The journey to Babyland is made by candle-light. You not only get there by candle-light, you get back again. That figures. I see a cottage bedroom with a candle burning.

To get to that supreme place, you have to have a good horse and bright spurs, or heels that are nimble and light. 'Bright' spurs shows that these are not real spurs. 'Sharp' spurs are real spurs. These give a prick in another sense. That other sense is the folk way of speaking. It survived up till the naming of Tottenham Hotspur Football Club. They are not a club of keen horse-riders or followers of Shakespeare's Harry Hotspur. They are like the rams who follow Derby County. They're hot diggety-dogs! Hot Dicky Delvers! Tottenham's symbol is the cock.

Back to our 'horse'. A 'good-ride' and a 'good gallop' can still mean riding bare-back, at night, with the candle burning. The heels still kick and drum.

How far is it to Babyland? It's a difficult question to

answer. We have three score miles and ten, or eight and eight, and other eight. It's a long way. Yet it isn't. It's just on and on and on and on. Till you come to a full-stop. Then your pen goes down.

How Many Miles to Babyland? (Restored)

'King and Queen of Cuntyland,
How many miles to Babyland?'
'Straight, and straight, and straight, and straight.'
'Can I get there by candle-light?'
'If your horse is strong, and your spurs are bright,
You can get there this very night.'

OTHER VERSIONS:

'Fucks-a-fucks, a bum all bare-y,
How many miles to lum all hairy?
Lum all flare-y.'
'Straight, and straight, and straight, and straight.'
'How shall I get in tonight.'
'Spin your balls and run up tight.'

'Prick my naggie, prick my naggie.
How many miles to have your Daddie?'
'Straight, and straight, and straight, and straight.'
'We'll not get there by candle-light.
Blow the canny candle out.'

High Diddle Diddle!
No. 213, ODNR

Hey diddle diddle,
The cat and the fiddle,
The cow jumped over the moon;
The little dog laughed
To see such sport,
And the dish ran away with the spoon.
(1765)

OTHER VERSIONS:

High diddle diddle . . .
The little dog laugh'd to see such craft
(1765)

And the maid ran away with the spoon, sir
(*c.* 1790)

And the dish lick't up the spoon
(1797)

On Saturday night I lost my wife
And where do you think I found her?
Up in the moon, singing a tune,
With all the stars around her.
(date ??)

But since ye think't an easy thing
To mount above the moon,
Of your own fiddle take a spring
And dance when ye have done.
(1597)

High diddle diddle! That's the tone of the rhyme-excited, playful. It's the fiddle playing, and it's the diddling of a fiddling instrument. For this is the famous fiddle of fiddles, on which good tunes will always be played. With a woman. She's the cat.

Then comes the key-phrase. 'The cow jumped over the moon'. 'Cow' still means woman—though it's become scornful. 'Jump' still means fuck. 'Over the moon' still means very happy. A woman was very happy after fucking.

After the woman's been happy, the little dog laughs. He's the man. 'Dog' for man, 'cat' for woman, is as old as 'They lead a cat and dog life.'

'To see such sport'—the act can be so very happy, and so overwhelming, that all little dogs can do, in public, is laugh at it and call it sport.

The 'dish' is the woman, again. ('She's a fine dish'). And the spoon is the stirrer, the dog, renamed. The woman ran off with the man.

The rhyme doesn't need much restoration. What it needs is understanding. It's a sort of code of imagery. But it's too cryptic. And the code is no longer current.

So I had to act as a folk-poet. I had to reveal the code by keeping on using it. That's the way all codes get broken. I kept on diddling.

High Diddle Diddle! (Restored)

High diddle diddle!
The cat and the fiddle!
The cow jumped over the moon!
The little dog laughed
To see such craft,
And the dish ran away with the spoon!

(Contd.)

High diddle diddle!
It is no riddle
To see a cow jump over the moon.
The dog played the fiddle
On the cat's middle,
And the dish was served with the spoon!

Cock A Doodle Doo!
No. 108, ODNR

Cock a doodle doo!
My dame has lost her shoe,
My master's lost his fiddlestick,
And knows not what to do.
                    (1765)

OTHER VERSIONS:

Cock a doodle doo,
What is my dame to do?
Till master finds his fiddling-stick
She'll dance without her shoe.

Cock a doodle doo,
My dame has found her shoe,
And master's found his fiddling-stick,
Sing doodle doodle doo.

Cock a doodle doo,
My dame will dance with you,
While master fiddles his fiddling-stick
For dame and doodle doo.
                    (1842)

Cock a doodle doo!
Dame has lost her shoe;
Gone to bed and scratch'd her head
And can't tell what to do.
                    (1853)

Cock-a-doodle-do,
My dad's gone to *ploo:*   *[plough]*
Mummy's lost her pudding-poke,
And knows not what to do.
                    (From Yorkshire, 1853?)

The song has been known since 1606 when its first
two lines were recorded. In 1800 its title was given as a
'Favourite Duet or Trio for Two or Three Voices,
Adapted for Juvenile Performers'.

Wake up! The cock's crowing. At the start of every
verse, too. He's telling us what kind of song we're
about to sing—a cock song.

'My dame has lost her shoe'. I don't know why 'shoe'
is a woman's sex-symbol. But it is. World-wide, too. 'A
worn slipper' is a Chinese phrase for a prostitute. Here
a shoe is still flung after brides at weddings. The
modern 'shoe' is 'bag'.

So 'My dame has lost her shoe' is impossible. Unless
she's turned into a mermaid. It's as impossible as 'My
master's lost his fiddlestick'. It can't have dropped off.
For 'fiddlestick's' meaning was shown in 'High Diddle
Diddle' and is revealed here again by calling it a
'pudding-poke'. That's because 'pudding' can mean
'belly', and 'poke' can mean 'poke'.

Two tragic losses, then, to begin? Because my dame
and my master have mislaid their wherewithals in
bed. 'Gone to bed and scratch'd her head.' So their pre-
dicament is funny. The cock crows that this is a funny
cock song.

It's bound to come (up) right in the end. Shoe and
fiddlestick can't be far away. The last line is 'For dame
and doodle doo'.

Juvenile performers can't. The song was spoiled when it was adapted for them in 1800. Now we can restore it to the Elizabethans, or to Ken Dodd. His tickling-stick is just the same as this fiddlestick.

Cock A Doodle Doo!
(Restored)

Cock a doodle doo!
My dame has lost her shoe!
My master's lost his fiddlestick!
They can't tell what to do!

Cock a doodle doo!
They're making much ado!
My dame looks for his fiddlestick!
My master for her shoe!

Cock a doodle doo!
They searched the whole bed through!
My dame has found his fiddlestick!
My master's found her shoe!

Cock a doodle doo!
My master wears her shoe!
My dame plays with his fiddlestick!
Now cock and doodle do!

Dear Missis Hubbard
No. 365, ODNR

Old Mother Hubbard
Went to the cupboard,
To fetch her poor dog a bone;
But when she came there
The cupboard was bare
And so the poor dog had none.

She went to the baker's
To buy him some bread;
But when she came back
The poor dog was dead.

She went to the undertaker's
To buy him a coffin;
But when she came back
The poor dog was laughing.

She took a clean dish
To get him some tripe;
But when she came back
He was smoking a pipe.

She went to the alehouse
To get him some beer;
But when she came back
The dog sat in a chair.

She went to the tavern
For white wine and red;
But when she came back
The dog stood on his head.

She went to the fruiterer's
To buy him some fruit;
But when she came back
He was playing the flute.

She went to the tailor's
To buy him a coat;
But when she came back
He was riding a goat.

She went to the hatter's
To buy him a hat;
But when she came back
He was feeding the cat.

She went to the barber's
To buy him a wig;
But when she came back
He was dancing a jig.

She went to the cobbler's
To buy him some shoes;
But when she came back
He was reading the news.

She went to the seamstress
To buy him some linen;
But when she came back
The dog was a-spinning.

She went to the hosier's
To buy him some hose;
But when she came back
He was dressed in his clothes.
(*contd.*)

The dame made a curtsy;
The dog made a bow;
The dame said Your servant,
The dog said Bow-wow.

(1805)

OTHER VERSIONS:

The above version was written down by Sarah Martin, but she claimed only the illustrations that were with it. 'Whether she merely added verses to a rhyme already known in oral tradition ... is still a subject for speculation', ODNR.

She went to the baker, To buy her some bread,
And when she came home, Her old husband was dead:

She went to the clerk to toll the bell,
And when she came home her old husband was well.

(1784)

The nursery rhyme is too long. It cannot be remembered. Yet it was known by heart, once. Why can't it be recalled?

It's had a whole second half, about clothing the dog, added on to it. The original was about feeding him, only. Then even that first half was made meaningless.

The dog. He's Mr. Hubbard. How do I know? First, because we still use 'dog' to mean 'man'. 'He's a gay dog.' This dog is Mrs. Hubbard's own dog. And dogs don't like bread, beer, wine and fruit—the foods Mrs. Hubbard buys. But men do. There is even an earlier version of the rhyme which states plainly, 'And when she came back, her old husband was well.'

Now, let us look at this dog's dinner. First, Mrs. Hubbard wants a bone for her poor dog. If 'dog' means 'man', 'bone' means 'erection'. It was still used like that when I went to school. 'Why did Mussolini send Mae West to Abyssinia?' 'To give General de Bono.' It was a real education!

When the cupboard's bare, there's no food to put the dog's back up. That's why he's poor. So Mrs. Hubbard goes out shopping. The first thing she buys—bread— is no good to dogs or men. It slays him—he lies down and curls up, the folk would say. But, after a daft undertaker-to-buy-a-coffin verse, she does buy stimulating foods. Tripe, beer, white wine and red, even fruit, are all fine foods for husbands. The dog plays the flute—should have been the French horn.

That was the folk-rhyme. How did it get all that second half about clothes added on to it? Because some lady, Miss Sarah Martin, didn't understand the first half. What a lady! She thought how easy it was to make a 'nonsense rhyme', so she just kept going when she came to write it down for the first time.

But her verses about clothes have no second meaning at all. They don't even have much of a first one! Look at

She went to the seamstress
To buy him some linen;
But when she came back
The dog was a-spinning.

The dog's spinning has no connection with buying him linen. Even the rhyme is bad.

Her verses don't join on to the feeding ones. We go straight from the fruiterer's, and the dog playing his flute, to the tailor's and the dog riding a goat. Such nonsensical verses do not carry the reader with them.

Nor do her verses end. They meander till they stop. Her last visit—to the hosier's—no more leads into the final 'The dame made a curtsy, The dog made a bow' than any other verse. No wonder the rhyme cannot be remembered.

Not only did she add the second half, she jumbled the first. It was she who wrote:

She went to the undertaker's
To buy him a coffin;
And when she came back
The poor dog was laughing.

She didn't know what she was writing about. So she wrote without rhyme or reason. Unless the sexual meaning is understood, there can be no reason for the dog's death and sudden resurrection.

Miss Martin could have gone on for ever! But what was she to do when she tired of rhyming? Simply stick the last verse from the folk-original back on the end! So she took

The dame made a curtsy,
The dog made a bow;
The dame said Your servant,
The dog said Bow-wow

from its rightful place, from following the dog eating fruit and playing the flute. There, he had been ready to play a good tune. His head nodded. His wife was ready to serve him. He said Woof! Woof! Think you can remember that?

Having detected Miss Martin's additions, I also discovered her subtractions. There should be more verses about the depressing foods, to balance the many on the stimulating ones. She remembered only bread, and killed the dog in the second verse. That's far too early. So I did my best to compose some. Unfortunately, my education finished too soon. I went to university.

However, I do know two more foods with a good,

modern, reputation. So I added them in, to keep the rhyme up to date.

And it's still too long! It doesn't matter. It has a good beginning and a good end. The middle play is as long as you wish.

Dear Missis Hubbard (Restored)

Dear Missis Hubbard
Went to the cupboard
To give her poor dog the bone;
But when she got there
The cupboard was bare
And so her poor dog didn't get one.

She went to the garden
And got him some peas;
And what she brought back
Made the dog weak at the knees.

She went to the well
And got him some water;
And what she brought back
Made the dog feel he was shorter.

She went to the oven
And got him some bread;
And what she brought back
Made the dog fall down dead.

THEN . . . she went to the tavern
And got white wine and red;
And what she brought back
Made the dog raise up his head.

She went to the poulterer's
And got him some eggs;
And what she brought back
Made the dog stretch out his legs.

She went to the butcher's
And got him some meat;
And what she brought back
Made the dog rise to his feet.

She went to the fruiterer's
And got him some fruit;
And what she brought back
Made the dog play on his flute.

She went to the fishmonger's
And got him some oysters;
And what she brought back
Made the dog become boisterous.

She went to the market
And got him some eels;
And what she brought back
Made the dog rock on his heels.

The dame made a curtsy,
The dog made a bow;
The dame said 'Your servant',
The dog said 'Bow-wow!'

The Mad Family
No. 327, ODNR

There was a mad man and he had a mad wife,
And they lived in a mad town:
And they had children three at a birth,
And mad they were every one.

The father was mad, the mother was mad,
And the children mad beside;
And they all got on a mad horse,
And madly they did ride.

They rode by night and they rode by day,
Yet never a one of them fell;
They rode so madly all the way,
Till they came to the gates of hell.

Old Nick was glad to see them so mad,
And gladly let them in:
But he soon grew sorry to see them so merry,
And let them out again.

(1760?)

OTHER VERSIONS:

It was a song, sung to great applause, in 1780.
The first printing (1744) shows the children
falling off the horse.

And they lived in a mad lane, Sir.

(1780)

If the song went 'They had ginger-haired twins at
every birth' would that make people pay attention?
Come on then. This couple had 'children three at

every birth'.

Mad, mad, mad, mad. Everything, everybody, is mad. What kind of horse is the mad horse? He gallops madly, right into hell. But its riders are so madly merry the Devil has to let them out again. They 'ride by night and they ride by day'. They ride all the time. That's what makes them mad. They have triplets at every birth.

There's only one mad horse that makes man and wife mad, and madly fertile. There's only one mad horse that it was supposed to be a sin to ride. It's the horse of sex 'raising its ugly head', as Victorians described it. There's the repression that sent the family to hell.

But the folk-rhyme let them out. For folk know that happy sexual love is happiness indeed. So, though they'd been told that the serpent in the Garden of Eden first raised its ugly head—condemning us all to death—their experience denied it. The serpent condemns us all to life!

Here we have the conflict between official culture and folk culture.

The folk still understood the song in 1780. That's why it was sung to great applause at some Palace of Varieties. The audience must have been able to see through, and enjoy, the words. Or, perhaps, a music-hall singer would dare sing the real ones, not the printed, official version.

For that's what we now have. The official censor interfered as soon as the song was printed, in 1744. He put 'Yet never a one of them fell'. But he didn't change the illustration! So, there are the children falling off the horse—and showing him up.

He, the first Great Victorian, obscured all the point of the song. In the second verse, he put that the mother was 'mad'. Yet the word should rhyme with 'horse'. So it should be the mother was 'worse'. Worse than the father! At once the song comes to life.

In the last verse, he tries to rhyme 'mad' and 'merry'. Well, he'd got rhymes inside the lines, and he must have hoped they'd cover the loss of rhyme at the line-ends. In the first verse, he'd already put 'in the mad town' instead of 'in the mad lane'. An insignificant difference? No, this mad riding is always done in a mad lane. It's one that has no turning! And once the right word is restored, the audience applaud.

Yet our censor left the mad man, the mad wife and the mad horse. He left the principals—without their principles! But—I've got six kids—two lots of three. My wife is more mad than I. We both know that our madness is the source of sanity.

Madly sane, I wanted to restore the lyric of our song. I'm immediately reminded of the folk who went out of a spring morning to clear the grass off the great horse on the white hill. I'm clearing the verbiage off the great horse on the white page.

The Mad Family
(Restored)

There was a mad man, and he had a mad wife,
And they lived in the mad lane;
They had children, three, every year of their life,
And mad they lived, the same.

The father was mad, the mother was worse,
The children more mad beside;
They'd all mount up on the great, mad horse,
And madly would they ride.

They rode all night and they rode all day,
They rode till dead they fell;
But they rose up madly, without stay,
And they rode to the gates of hell.

Old Nick was glad to see them so mad,
And gladly he let them in;
But they rode so bad on his poor old pad
That he let them out again!

Ladybird, Ladybird, Fly Away Home
No. 296, ODNR

Ladybird, Ladybird,
Fly away home,
Your house is on fire
And your children all gone.
All except one
And that's little Ann
And she has crept under
The warming pan.

(1840?)

OTHER VERSIONS:
Your children will burn
(1744)

There are similar rhymes from Germany,
Denmark, Sweden, Switzerland and France.
A German version is 'Heaven's little cow, fly away!
Your house is on fire, your children are all crying.' A
French one is 'Fly into the blue sky. Your nest is on fire.
The Turks, with their swords, are going to kill your
brood.'

Tom Wakefield remembered a rhyme about a ladybird
from his boyhood in Staffordshire:

Ladybird, Ladybird,
I'll bring you some money.
Ladybird, Ladybird,
Give me some honey.

'Mother, fly home. Danger is threatening your children.' That's the cry of all the versions. But our English rhyme has added that little Ann has crept under the warming-pan and is, presumably, saved. That is sentimental, babyish and too late. For warming-pans were used in seventeenth- and eighteenth-century England, long after the rhyme was composed. The German version shows that the Anglo-Saxons brought it with them to England in the fifth century.

They were pagan. They called the ladybird 'Heaven's little cow'. For them, as for Hindus, the cow and the mother must have been connected. For the ladybird has many children. In France she has a whole brood of them. She is a wife and mother symbol—what we, in England, call a home-bird. Some commentators try to make her into 'Our Lady's bird'. There's a babyish, sentimental and too late gloss about that, as well. For there are many names where lady means woman: Ladies' Bed Straw was where many women lay, and became mothers. The piece of lore I remember about ladybirds from my childhood was that if one landed on a girl, she would become pregnant, not religious. Christianity came late to the Anglo-Saxons.

Back to Europe. Why do all the rhymes tell such dreadful lies? Surely her house is not on fire. (Whoever heard of a real ladybird with a house?) Surely the Turks haven't landed in France?

The mother is needed. She must fly home as quickly as possible. The worse the lies, the faster she will fly. We used to blow on her, to make her start off. Why get her home? Because that's where the woman's place is, when she's got little children. We think they need her love. Then they needed her protection against all sorts of dangers.

Her husband needs her too! The Staffordshire working-man, perhaps a miner, wants her home to love him.

But she is not just a house-wife, she's a house-goddess! For the ladybird has always had 'sacred associations'. The rhyme is 'possessed of awful significance'. It has been thought 'a relic of Freya worship' (ODNR).

Freya was Frig, the goddess of mother-making, on the Ladies' Bed Straw. Frig was goddness of flowers, as well as of frigging. She was worshipped on Friday—Friga's day. Now the Ladies' Bed Straw, the Heaven's Little Cow and the Great Mother fly back home to us, from our pagan past, with wife-and-mother love.

Ladybird, Ladybird, Fly Away Home (Restored)

Ladybird, ladybird,
Fly away home,
Your house is on fire
And your children will burn.

Ladybird, ladybird,
Fly away, fly,
They all of them need you
Out of the sky.

Ladybird, ladybird,
Mother of all,
Stay by the fire-side,
No ill shall befall.

Robin the Bobbin' (1)

No. 454, ODNR

Robin the Bobbin, the big-bellied Ben,
He ate more meat than fourscore men;
He ate a cow, he ate a calf,
He ate a butcher and a half,
He ate a church, he ate a steeple,
He ate the priest and all the people!
A cow and a calf,
An ox and a half,
A church and a steeple,
And all the good people,
And yet he complained that his stomach wasn't full.

(c. 1830)

OTHER VERSIONS:

He ate the minister off his staff,
He licked the ladle, he swallowed the spoon,
And wasna' fu' when a' was done.

(1901, Scots)

He swallit the kirk,
He swallit the queir,
He swallit the meenister's
Auld grey mare.

(1948)

The belief has been expressed several times that the rhyme refers to the rapacious nature of Henry VIII in seizing Church estates (ODNR).

An enormous Robin! The rhyme tells of huge sexual desires, not of their human limitations. Robin is god-like, tall as a giant, tall as the church steeple, where the cock still stands.

He is not Henry VIII. Only six wives! Henry did become a folk-figure because of his brutal treatment of women. He was a Mr Punch with a beheading axe. But he was not remembered by the folk for his appetite for Church lands.

Robin's rhyme can be rightly restored by reasoning. He will not eat men. Consequently, 'butcher and a half', 'priest and all the people' and 'an ox and a half' are all wrong. They are substitutes for female dishes.

But neither will he eat bread and butter! He wants food that will 'put your back up', as the folk say. Church and choir don't do anything for him. It's the proud, strong nourishment he wants, like the 'steeple', 'staff', 'ladle' and 'spoon' he gets when his rhyme is correctly remembered. He wants to be plain as a pikestaff.

So, much of his diet has been forgotten. The form of the second half of the verse confirms the forgetting. Four of the lines are too short, the last is too long. Someone wasn't very good at making it up.

But we can help Robin make it up. We can add modern refreshments to stimulate his resurrection. That will be his life—to eat contemporary foods—for he lives in every time. Robin rules, OK?

Robin the Bobbin' (1) (Restored)

Robin the Bobbin', the big-bellied Ben,
Stuffed more tuck than a hundred men.
He ate a tart and then a crumpet,
He ate a slice from off the brisket.

He ate a pigeon, then a hen,
He ate a bitch, and then a vixen.
He ate a filly, then a mare,
He ate a cow, and then three more.
He ate a tower, and then a steeple,
In the belfry were the people,
He ate the chitterling on the table,
He cracked the dish, then licked the ladle.
He wasn't full when all was done,
But stood, and looked for more to come.

Robin the Bobbin' (2)
No. 449, ODNR

Robin-a-bobbin
He bent his bow,
Shot at a pigeon
And killed a crow;
Shot at another
And killed his own brother,
Did Robin-a-bobbin
Who bent his bow.

(1853)

OTHER VERSIONS:

Shoot again, and kill a wren,
And that will do for gentlemen.

(1892)

There was a little one-eyed gunner,
Who killed all the birds that died last summer.

(1844)

This is a rhyme for the reasonable men. That first
Robin was too much for them. This second one shoots
only four women—the pigeon, the crow, 'his own
brother' and the wren (Other Version). That's reasonable—by folk standards. 'If you can't shoot six women,
you can't shoot at all,' as young men sing.

'His own brother' is, of course, wrong. Cock Robin
shoots hen-birds. His usual target is the wren. But
young pouter pigeons and old, painted crows may fall
to his arrow. So 'his own brother' can be corrected to
'her own mother'.

'And that will do for gentlemen.' After he's shot the wren, his bow won't bend any more. He'll stop bobbing. The first Robin the Bobbin' would say 'He's been filled to the top of his bent.'

Robin the Bobbin' (2) (Restored)

Robin the Bobbin'
Bent his bow,
Shot at a pigeon
And killed a crow;
Shot at another
And killed her mother.
He shot again,
Killed a wren.
That's enough, then
For all us men.

Other Versions: Not so little!

There was a little one-eyed gunner
Who shot all the birds that died last summer!

Who Killed Cock Robin?
No. 110, ODNR

Who killed Cock Robin?
I, said the Sparrow,
With my bow and arrow,
I killed Cock Robin.

Who saw him die?
I, said the Fly,
With my little eye,
I saw him die.

Who caught his blood?
I, said the Fish,
In my little dish,
I caught his blood.

Who'll make the shroud?
I, said the Beetle,
With my thread and needle,
I'll make the shroud.

Who'll dig his grave?
I, said the Owl,
With my pick and shovel,
I'll dig his grave.

Who'll be the parson?
I, said the Rook,
With my little book,
I'll be the parson.

Who'll be the clerk?
I, said the Lark,
If it's not in the dark,
I'll be the clerk.

Who'll carry the link?
I, said the Linnet,
I'll fetch it in a minute,
I'll carry the link.

Who'll be chief mourner?
I, said the Dove,
I mourn for my love,
I'll be chief mourner.

Who'll carry the coffin?
I, said the Kite,
If it's not through the night,
I'll carry the coffin.

Who'll bear the pall?
We, said the Wren,
Both the cock and the hen,
We'll bear the pall.

Who'll sing a psalm?
I, said the Thrush,
As she sat on a bush,
I'll sing a psalm.

Who'll toll the bell?
I, said the Bull,
Because I can pull,
I'll toll the bell.

All the birds of the air
Fell a-sighing and a-sobbing,
When they heard the bell toll
For poor Cock Robin.

(1788)

OTHER VERSIONS:

All the birds of the air
Fell a-sighin' and a-sobbin'
When they heard of the death
Of poor Cock Robin,
When they heard of the death
Of poor Cock Robin.

(Modern Chorus)

There are related rhymes from other countries. The Spanish is: 'Who has died? John, the one-eyed. Who bewails him? His lady love. Who sings for him? Her throat. Who cries for him? His child.'

The Italian is: 'Who had died? Beccotorto. Who has sounded the bell? That mischievous clown.'

The German rhyme is: 'Who is dead? Breadless. When will he be buried? On the eve of the day after tomorrow, with spades and shovels. The Cuckoo is the grave-digger, the Stork is the bell-ringer, the Pee-wit acts as scholar, with all his sisters and brothers.'

Who killed Cock Robin? Whoever composed that rhyme! For he changed a folk-song about Man into a political rhyme about a man. Soon his political references were forgotten, dead and buried. Cock Robin, as a politician, is a dead duck.

Let's resurrect him and see him sit up on a garden spade!

There are two theories about this rhyme. The first is that it is a political rhyme about the intrigues to dismiss Robert Walpole, the Prime Minister, in 1740. The sparrow represents the chief plotter, and the other birds are part of the group which 'buried' Walpole.

The second theory is that it comes from some early myth and is part of European folk-culture. It was then rewritten in Walpole's time.

I am of that second opinion. The previous restorations show that there are other rhymes about man and woman told through birds. The 'Other Versions' from Europe show that it does form part of 'European folk-culture'. What that means is that the song is pagan.

'Pagan' in the sense of being about sex. The European rhymes all are. The Spanish one calls Robin 'John the one-eyed'—like the 'little one-eyed gunner'. The Italian calls him 'Crooked Beak'. The German says he is 'Breadless'—all meat! Putting the three together, Robin must be phallic. His lady-love bewails him. Her throat sings for him. Cuckoldry is his gravedigger. The stork is the bell-ringer. And little Peesy-Weesy is the learner.

All Europe tells of the death of male potency. Would all Europe bother with the fall of the British Prime Minister? Where's the song about Pitt?

We have to reconnect 'Who Killed Cock Robin' to British, and European, folklore. We have extensive changes to make, because the political rewriting was extensive.

First, the sparrow is not the killer. There is no British or European pairing of Robin and Sparrow. But there is a British pairing of Robin and Wren. The wren was the last bird Robin killed in 'Robin the Bobbin' (2). He killed her, and she killed him!

To relate the symbolism to real life, there is only one bird that can 'kill' the phallus, and that is the woman-bird.

The second sign of change is that all the actors should be birds. They start at verse five and act on till the end—verse thirteen. But verse two has the fly, verse three the fish, and verse four the beetle. That's the whole start of the rhyme changed.

Why? Because the political rhymer wants to go on about the burial. Yet the theme is 'Who Killed Cock Robin?' Not 'Who Buried Him?'

Having changed the question, he's left with no real end to his rhyme. 'Who'll toll the bell?' is no more an end than 'Who'll bear the pall?' or 'Who'll carry the coffin?'

Nor will his symbolism fit. By what right has the Sparrow got a bow and arrow, the Fish a little dish, the Beetle a thread and needle, the Owl a pick and shovel? Only by the right of rhyme! And, being charitable, because the real politicians known as the Sparrow, the Fish etc. were identifiable by them. But a real rhyme's symbolism does fit.

Given that the satirist altered a lot, what did he leave? First, he left some of the birds' names. That would tie his rhyme in with the old original. Robert Walpole must have been known as Cock Robin. And he kept some of the rhymes: 'I, said the Lark/If it's not in the dark.' That's a senseless thing to say about a funeral. But it's not senseless if it refers to man and woman. 'I, said the Dove/I mourn for my love.' 'I, said the Thrush/As she sat on a bush.' As part of a political satire, that's not very sparkling. But, as part of a sexual song, it twinkles.

But some birds' names don't fit at all. The bullfinch, to pull, must be all wrong, because we want female birds to kill Robin, not male ones. And the pair of wrens to bear the pall must be all wrong, too, as we want one wren to be the final killer.

But the chorus is still the original one. It keeps the tone of the old song. It's half-serious, mock-serious, as the killing of the wren with bow and arrow was only half-serious. For you can't keep a good man down! Robin resurrects. So the birds are only 'a-sighing and a-sobbing, when they heard of the death . . .'. Of the 'death', sing the folk, not of the burial.

Putting all together, for our reconstruction, we have the theme, the foreknowledge of who the killer was, of some of the other birds involved, of the tone of the song, and its chorus.

Logic will take us further. The real killer, the wren, must come at the end of the song. The other birds must come before her and claim to have done the deed, as only then could the chorus come in with 'All the birds of the air/Fell a-sighin' and a-sobbin' '. Each claim must be shown to be wrong, and so lead on to the next bird's claim. There has to be a comic-serious twist to the end to fit the tone, and underlying meaning, of the song.

This reconstruction must be a long shot. The current rhyme is meaningless, on any level. All its meaning has to be put back. Robin the Bobbin' must bend his long bow, and shoot a wren a long way away. He has tried to put his arrow near the others, near the other folk-rhymes from Britain and Europe. If the reconstruction takes life from them, and gives life to them, then, 'That's enough for all us men', as Robin the Bobbin said. He won't be dead and buried in a Nursery Rhyme book.

Who Killed Cock Robin?
(Restored)

Men:
Who killed Cock Robin?

Woman Solo:
'I' said the lark,
'When it was dark,'
I killed Cock Robin.'

Women:
All the birds of the air
Fell a-sighin' and a-sobbin'
When they heard of the death
Of poor Cock Robin,
When they heard of the death
Of poor Cock Robin.

Men:
No, you did not!
He rose after that.
Who killed Cock Robin?

Woman solo:
'I' said the dove
'With my coo of love,
I killed Cock Robin.'

Women:
All the birds of the air
Fell a-sighin' and a-sobbin'
When they heard of the death
Of poor Cock Robin,
When they heard of the death
Of poor Cock Robin.

Men:
No, you did not!
He rose after that.
Who killed Cock Robin?

Woman solo:
'I' said the finch,
'With my pull and pinch,
I killed Cock Robin.'

Women:
All the birds of the air *etc.*

Men:
No, you did not!
He rose after that.
Who killed Cock Robin?

Woman solo:
'I' said the thrush
'With my little bush,
I killed Cock Robin.'

Women:
All the birds of the air *etc.*

Men:
No, you did not!
He rose after that.
Who killed Cock Robin?

Woman solo:
'Not I' said the wren,
'I asked him in.
I didn't kill him.'

Men:
Yes, but you did!
His red breast is hid.
You killed Cock Robin.

Women:
All the birds of the air *etc.*

Men:
He is not slain!
He's risen again!

Men and Women:
All the birds of the air
Fell a-singin' and a-songin'
When they heard of the rise
Of proud Cock Robin,
When they heard of the rise
Of proud Cock Robin.

Initiation
No. 82, ODNR

Buff says Buff to all his men,
And I say Buff to you again;
Buff neither laughs nor smiles,
But carries his face,
With a very good grace,
And passes the stick to the very next place.
                                        (1831)

OTHER VERSIONS:

'Knock, knock!'   [*Thumping floor with stick.*]
'Who's there?'
'Buff.'
'What says Buff?'
'Buff says Buff to all his men,
And I say Buff to you again.'
'Methinks Buff smiles.'
'Buff neither laughs nor smiles,
But looks in your face [or 'strokes his face']
With a comical grace
And delivers the staff to you, sir.'
                                        (1883?)

'My father sent me here with a staff,
To speak to you and not to laugh.'
'Methinks you smile.' 'Methinks I don't.
I smooth my face with ease and grace,
And set my staff in its proper place.'
                                        (1883)

In the German folk version, the child in the middle of
the circle says (my translation): 'I went across the
churchyard. There, a Bishop met me. The Bishop he

106

was young and handsome. He did not like to be alone, the Bishop, the Bishop, the Bishop.' He strikes with a stick in front of one of the children in the circle, who steps forward and says, 'Father Everhard [Eberhard, in German] I take you by thy venerable beard. If you see me laugh, I will watch in your place.' Also, a speaker—it's not so clear who it is—says, 'I am the Lord of Right, I forbid laughing and talking. Who laughs or speaks must pay forfeit.'

ODNR says this is 'an old forfeits game. The players seat themselves in a circle, and one, taking a wand, points it at his neighbour, repeating the rhyme with mock solemnity. The player pointed at then becomes the one who points, and so on, round the circle. Those who laugh or smile must pay a forfeit.'

When it was old, it was not a game! It was a serious custom. As time passed, and beliefs were changed, it became a modern forfeits game for children.

For this rhyme is very old, as the German version shows. It was being said before the Angles and Saxons sailed to what became Angle-land, before they were Christianized and customs converted.

This one shows an initiation ceremony. The speaker in the middle of the ring, Father Everhard, is the leader, the 'magician', who is met when someone goes across the churchyard, the place of the ancestors. The children sitting round him are his confirmation class—the young men to be instructed in the meaning of adult sexuality. It is because this lesson is so important that none of the initiates must laugh or speak. The lesson he teaches concerns his staff—the staff of life. The young men must take it gravely and pass it on.

The German version suggests that the magician is now called the Bishop. Perhaps the Bishop's crook was once the staff of Buff? The touching of the beard, as a sign of sexual closeness, is both old and current. I saw two engraved Assyrians greeting each other by touching each other's beards—and the French still say '*Oh, la barbe!*'

The clinching detail is the name of this ancestor-magician. 'Buff' means a buffet, a blow or stroke; and also, it means naked. Buff says 'Be naked' to all his men, 'Strike a good blow.'

Initiation Passing on the Staff (Restored)

Buff: 'Knock, Knock!' [*thumps with staff*]
1st Lad: 'Who's there?'
Buff: 'Buff. I am the lord of all that's upright.
               Who smiles or laughs must pay forfeit.'
1st Lad: 'What says Buff?'
Buff: 'Buff will never be alone.
                Buff says "Bare Buff" to all his men.'
1st Lad: 'And I say "Bare Buff" to you again.
               Father Ever-hard,
               I take you by the bushy beard.
               If you see me laugh
               While I take your staff
               You may make me affeared.'
Buff: 'Methinks you smile.'
1st Lad: 'Methinks I don't.
               I keep a straight face
               While I thump in this place; [*Thumps staff*]
               And I pass back the staff
               With a serious grace
               To the lord of this place.'
[*Hands staff back to Buff, who recommences the dialogue with the next lad.*]

When Buff has catechized each of the lads, he would say something like this:

All of you are now my men.
I will come to you again
At your great need.
Thump with your own staff then.
I'll help indeed.

Oranges and Lemons

No. 392, ODNR

Oranges and lemons,
Say the bells of St Clement's.

You owe me five farthings,
Say the bells of St Martin's.

When will you pay me?
Say the bells of Old Bailey.

When I grow rich,
Say the bells of Shoreditch.

When will that be?
Say the bells of Stepney.

I'm sure I don't know,
Says the great bell at Bow.

Here comes a candle to light you to bed,
Here comes a chopper to chop off your head.

(1858)

OTHER VERSIONS:

The song's earliest recording is:

Two Sticks and Apple,
Ring ye Bells at Whitechapple,
Old Father Bald Pate,
Ring ye Bells Aldgate, *etc.*

(*c.*1744)

The longest version contains:

Halfpence and farthings,
Say the bells of St Martin's.
Kettles and pans,
Say the bells of St Ann's.
Brickbats and tiles,
Say the bells of St Giles.
Old shoes and slippers,
Say the bells of St Peter's.
Pokers and tongs,
Say the bells of St John's.
                        (1805)

The ending couplet is given as:

Pancakes and fritters
Say the bells of St Peter's.
                        (1810)

The earliest record of the name 'Oranges and
Lemons' was as a square-for-eight dance, in 1665.
   The game, accompanying the song, is described in
ODNR: 'Two of the bigger players determine in secret
which of them shall be an "orange" and which a
"lemon"; they then form an arch by joining hands and
sing the song while the others in a line troop under-
neath. When the two players who form the arch
approach, with quickening tempo, the climax of their
recitation . . . they repeat ominously "Chop, chop,
chop, chop, CHOP!" and on the last CHOP they bring
their arms down around whichever child is at that
moment passing under the arch. The captured player
is asked privately whether he will be an "orange" or a
"lemon" (alternatively a "plum pudding" or "roast
beef"; "tart" or "cheese-cake"; a "sack of corn" or
"sack of coals") and he goes to the back of the player

he finds he has chosen . . . As now usually played, the end comes when every child has been lined up on one or other side of the arch, whereupon there is a tug of war . . . '

The questions and answers, as in 'London Bridge', indicate a dialogue. Who is it between?

Let's summarize the song. There is, in most versions, a number of joined images: 'Oranges and lemons', 'Two sticks and apple', 'Halfpence and farthings' etc. Then, 'You owe me . . . ' 'When will you pay?' 'When I grow rich' 'When?' 'Don't know' 'Candle to bed' 'Chopper to chop off your head.'

The end is the clearest part. It's about going to bed. The head being chopped off there must be a maidenhead. Because you don't really execute people in bed. So the 'chopper' must be a metaphor, as in the current slang 'a chopper-flasher'. That understanding is confirmed by the 'Chop, chop, chop, chop, CHOP.' It is no real execution.

Now we can deduce who the dialogue is between. The only group that can sing 'Here comes a chopper etc' is the lads' group. Only the girls can sing 'Here comes a candle to light you to bed.' They are provoking the lads.

Now we know how the song is ending, it is much easier to make sense of the middle and the beginning. The beginning, those joined images, is either male or female pairs. The clearest of all is 'old shoes and slippers' for girls, as those are still flung after brides; then, the 'pokers and tongs' for the boys, because of the pun. 'Old Father Bald Pate' seems an obvious description of the phallus. Some of the others— 'orange', 'kettle' and 'pancake'—are given as symbols of the female part in Partridge's *Dictionary of Slang*. These symbolic descriptions of either sex are sung to provoke and stimulate.

Having sufficiently aroused each other—we see that the number of 'insults' is not fixed—the song proceeds to the question of some debt and its payment. That calling to account must be symbolic, because its conclusion is bed, and no real debts of trifling amounts lead there. (I know about the coalman who finished his day shouting 'Coal for money.') The lads owe the girls five far-things. They will pay when they are rich in potency.

When the girls ask 'When will that be?' the recorded answer is 'I'm sure I don't know.' But the song demands a sure answer here, not a hesitant one. For the girls, on receiving it, go straight to 'Here comes a candle to light you to bed.' They would not have issued such an invitation if the lads 'didn't know'. The original must have had the meaning 'Now!', and so befit the *great* bell of Bow which gives it.

Orange and Lemons (Restored)

Lads: 'Orange and lemons'
         Say the bells of St Clement's.

Girls: 'Two pips and an apple'
         Say the bells of Whitechapel.

Lads: 'Old shoe and slippers'
         Say the bells of St Peter's.

Girls: 'Poker and tongs'
         Say the bells of St John's.

Lads: 'Bull's eye and targets'
         Say the bells of St Margaret's.

Girls: 'Old Father Bald Pate'
Say the bells at the Aldgate.

Lads: 'I owe you five farthings'
Say the bells of St Martin's.

Girls: 'When will you pay me?'
Say the bells of Old Bailey.

Lads: 'When I grow rich'
Says the bells of Shoreditch.

Girls: 'When will that be?'
Say the bells of Stepney.

Lads: 'My time is now!'
Says the great bell of Bow.

Girls: 'Then here comes a candle to light
you to bed.'

Lads: 'And here comes a chopper to chop off your
head!'

Together: 'Chop, chop, chop, chop, CHOP!'

Note: 'Orange and lemons' is altogether a female symbol (one orange and two lemons: a 'three' of woman's sexual parts). Therefore, the caught player cannot be asked if he, or she, is 'Orange' or 'Lemon'. That is a modern misunderstanding. But 'Sack of coal, or sack of corn?' should be asked; or, alternatively, 'Plum-pudding or roast beef?' For those questions are also recorded in the Other Versions—and they do make sense: which side are you on, in the sex tug-of-war? Thus, the line-up becomes all lads against all girls. The outcome is then inevitable, but desired.

114

Old Roger was Dead

From the *Puffin Book of Nursery Rhymes**

Old Roger is dead and laid in his grave,
Laid in his grave, laid in his grave,
Old Roger is dead and laid in his grave,
H'm ha! laid in his grave.

They planted an apple tree over his head,
Over his head, over his head,
They planted an apple tree over his head,
H'm ha! over his head.

The apples grew ripe and ready to fall,
Ready to fall, ready to fall,
The apples grew ripe and ready to fall,
H'm ha! ready to fall.

There came an old woman a-picking them all,
A-picking them all, a-picking them all,
There came an old woman a-picking them all,
H'm ha! a-picking them all.

Old Roger jumps up and gives her a knock,
Gives her a knock, gives her a knock,
Which makes the old woman go hippety-hop,
H'm ha! hippety-hop.

Every verse, except the last, has only one statement.
But the last verse has two. So this last verse has been
altered. It should be two verses. Further, the second of
them, based on 'Which makes the old woman go
hippety-hop', is suspect. The rhyme between 'hop' and
'knock' is a bad one. It's an attempt to link together
this alteration, to make up another ending which will
more-or-less rhyme.

*Gathered by Iona and Peter Opie, Puffin Books, 1963

115

It is possible to deduce what the true ending is, from the story. 'Old Roger is dead and laid in his grave. They planted an apple tree over his head. The apples grew ripe and ready to fall. There came an old woman a-picking them all. Old Roger jumps up and gives her a knock [alteration]. Which makes the old woman go hippety-hop [alteration].' When the woman comes picking the apples, Roger revives, jumps up, and . . . So there are two significant actions, which lead to the revival, the apples growing ripe, and the coming of the woman picking them. What do they symbolize? They have to symbolize something, or a realistic resurrection will be religious!

Apples growing ripe and ready to fall are male fruit ready for plucking. The apple-tree has been a male symbol before, in 'Upon Paul's Steeple'. That is why it was chosen to be planted over Old Roger's head. It fitted him capitally. For who is Old Roger? He is John Thomas, King Dick or any other contemporary name. I know a rhyme about him which tells how he, the lodger, seduced the landlady's daughter. The apples' ripening shows that his potency has returned.

The woman comes picking all his fruit. She is not old, any more than he is. 'Old women' in nursery rhymes are any age between sixteen and sixty. He arouses and 'gives her a knock', which makes the woman do something or other, which follows his potent blow. Whatever it was, it rhymed with the preceding verse. The nursery rhyme tried to preserve that rhyming link between verses, in the same way as 'ready to fall' rhymes with 'a-picking them all'. So the verse we have to restore has a predictable content and form.

But then the rhyme didn't end! It stopped. To become a poem, it needs to answer 'Old Roger is dead and laid in his grave.' It needs a triumphant conclusion. So I composed one more verse, my original composition, which—as always—the reader may accept or reject. There is no justification for it in the text of the nursery rhyme. Only sense and feeling demand it.

I learned that when the rhyme is said by children, they chorus the second and fourth lines of each verse. I accept that, for the form is too repetitive to be said by one speaker only. They also act the rhyme, with Roger dead in the middle of a circle, and a girl coming to pick the apples. It does seem to me that they are keeping up an old ceremonial poem, about the death and rebirth of male potency, linked up with seasonal fruitfulness, and revival. I imagine the poem said by some pagan leader, chorused by the villagers, at New Year to link the sun's revival with man's own potency.

When it was said in a pub, I found the Wassailers much preferred a boisterous 'Oooh! Aaah! to the Puffin book's 'H'm ha!', so I accepted their emendation. The folk have the last word.

Old Roger was* Dead ... (Restored)

Old Roger lay down, Old Roger was dead,
Old Roger was dead, Old Roger was dead,
Old Roger lay down, Old Roger was dead,
[*Chorus*] Ooh! Aah! Old Roger was dead.

They planted an apple-tree over his head,
Over his head, over his head,
They planted an apple-tree over his head,
[*Chorus*] Ooh! Aah! over his head.

The apples grew ripe and ready to fall,
Ready to fall, ready to fall,
The apples grew ripe and ready to fall,
[*Chorus*] Ooh! Aah! ready to fall.

117

There came a young woman a-picking them all,
A-picking them all, a-picking them all,
There came a young woman a-picking them all,
[*Chorus*] Ooh! Aah! a-picking them all.

Old Roger jumps up and gives her a thwack,
Gives her a thwack, gives her a thwack,
Old Roger jumps up and gives her a thwack,
[*Chorus*] Ooh! Aah! gives her a thwack.

Which lays the young woman down on her back,
Down on her back, down on her back,
Which lays the young woman down on her back,
[*Chorus*] Ooh! Aah! down on her back.

Old Roger lives! He still has the knack,
He still has the knack, he still has the knack,
Old Roger lives! He still has the knack,
[*Chorus*] Ooh! Aah! he still has the knack.

*The change of tense—from the past to the present—is in the nursery
rhyme. It shows that the rhyme is acted as it is being said.

Carols

'These were the originals from which the published songs had been derived, but they were so appallingly bawdy that, as they rang out over the river, I was lost in admiration for the ingenuity of the folk-song collector who had managed to twist and trim the lyrics so that they became printable.'
DAVID ATTENBOROUGH, *Zoo Quest To Guyana.*

'What appeared to have happened was that some monk in Canterbury in the eleventh or twelfth century had got at a copy of the Anglo-Saxon Chronicle and inserted various items of false history, usually to the effect that someone had died, and left his lands to the See of Canterbury.'
R. V. JONES, *Most Secret War.*

Introduction
'A happy holly and a merry berry!'

ARGUMENT

1. That some of the traditional carols come from the pagan Yule festival.
2. That they survived till about 1350–1450.
3. That then they, together with secular songs, were altered by Churchmen.
4. That they can be restored by consideration of the altered parts, as well as of the unaltered.

Why does Father Christmas wear a red cloak? Why is he Father Christmas and not Mother Christmas? Once we begin to question the meaning of our Christmas customs, we find the answers in the pagan past. Nearly everything we do at Christmas—decorating the tree with fairy lights, filling the children's stockings, eating turkey and mince-pie—has grown from the pre-Christian festival.

We turn to the *Encyclopaedia Britannica*, the scientific Bible, and it reveals

'December 25th was the date of a pagan festival, chosen in AD 274 by the Emperor Hadrian, as the Sun's Birthday. December 17th to the 24th was the Roman Saturnalia, a time of merry-making and exchange of presents. On January 1st, houses were decorated with greenery and lights, and presents were given to the poor and to children. To these Roman rites were added the Germano-Celtic Yule rites. Special food and good fellowship, the Yule log and Yule cakes, greenery and fir trees, wassailing, gifts and greetings, all commemorated different aspects of the festive season. Fires and lights, symbols of warmth and everlasting life, have always been associated with the Winter festival.'

121

Crown of Horns

Another quotation, from Chambers' *Encyclopaedia,* helps to clear the mind wonderfully: 'There is no authoritative tradition as to the day or month of Christ's birth.'

Father Christmas is not St. Nicholas or Santa Claus, for here the *Encyclopaedia Britannica* furnishes us with a negative: 'His [St. Nicholas'] existence is not testified by any historical document.' Who is he then, this old man with white beard, who comes from the north, driving reindeer? He is Odin, father of the Norse gods, who used to come on dark and stormy nights to reward or punish his worshippers (from *A Year of*

Festivals, Palmer and Lloyd). And that's why my parents told me I'd get a stockingful of ashes if I had not been good! That's why he isn't Mother Christmas!

The red cloak has to be deduced. As Odin comes in mid-winter, its scarlet must relate to the sun's return, to the symbols of warmth and everlasting life of which Britannica spoke. The colour is the same as the holly berry's colour, the same symbolic colour as the red, red Robin in the snow. It is fire and life-blood.

People are thinking not only of the rebirth of the sun, they are thinking of themselves, of the stress of living in winter. That is why they call the sun Unconquered. They don't want to be overcome by dark and cold. The sun is their warrior hero, his title the one they most admire. Nature is not science but sympathy.

Christianity has no customs. How would anyone know how to celebrate the return of the sun, the coming of spring flowers or the gathering of harvest from the New Testament? So the Yule customs were taken over, with the explanation of them changed. 'St Nicholas and Odin have become the same person' (*A Year of Festivals*). 25 December is 'of course' the birthday of the Sun of Righteousness! (If only I knew what that was.) Unfortunately for the changers, the Romans could write. The Druids and the Norse could not.

The customs were taken over, rather than destroyed, because of the difficulty of destroying human nature. Joy that the days are going to get longer, and warmer, that spring will eventually come, is very deep-rooted. The pubs are full of people celebrating it. The Anglo-Saxons were going to church on 25 December to sing and dance, as Bede records. How much easier, how much cleverer, to keep the place, the day and the form but change the meaning!

The church-sites were taken over. Notre Dame was built on top of a church to a river goddess, whose altar was in the cathedral foundations. The evidence was removed, and is now safely in the Musée de Cluny, Paris. The word was changed too. Pagan churches became temples. St Paul's was the 'temple' of Diana. Who, one wonders, was the original god of Canterbury Cathedral? For the Christian church has managed to bury, in its foundations, many of the altars it is built upon. Only some, like some of the carols, are preserved.

The main services of the Sun's Day had naturally been at dawn, noon and sunset, the time of three of the present church services. Carolling has a special part in the midnight service on Christmas Eve. Was a baby born then, or the sun?

Other songs, sacred to Hymen, goddess of marriage, became hymns, presumably ancient as well as modern. Easter, the celebration of Eastra, goddess of spring, became the time of Christ's unspringing. So every practice and custom was combined with some approximate Christian belief, and survived under its different cover.

The Earth-Mother herself—from whom so many goddesses spring—is outside most Catholic churches, still with a child in her arms.

Wassailing is named by the *Encyclopaedia Britannica* as part of the Yule festival. *'Waes Heil'* was what the Vikings said: 'Be in health.' When British drinkers say 'Good health', they are repeating the toast of their Norse ancestors. To go around wishing neighbours good health was to go a-wassailing, 'among the leaves so green'. The wassailers were carrying the greenery—and the lights—with them. The children going round carolling today, are really wassailing.

The survival of the wassails shows that songs can, indeed, last from pagan times till now. They have changed language, from old Norse to modern English, as the people changed. They changed verse form. Like

124

the proverbs, many of which came from Germany, they changed their grammar. The wassails are living fossils. But then we, too, are living fossils.

They are the songs which no missionary worked over. They are classed, now, in the *Oxford Book of Carols*, as 'Christmas, secular', whereas, of course, they are 'New Year, religious'. But these acknowledged escapees still suffered, because they were from the old, pagan culture. They were like gypsies or Red Indians—survivors, but unwanted. So the wassails have become ever more beggarly, ever more repressed, as the wassailers felt the hostility of the new restrictive society. The wishes were not only for good-health, but for fertility, for sexual joy. And so the singers gradually became shame-faced. They were the poor, the uneducated; and the rich and the genteel thought them rude. The songs survived among farm-labourers, with words disguised from the gentleman-farmer and the educated folk-song collector. When a culture is under attack, it tries to keep itself secret and appears in dark places, in those few environments which are not repressed. I found my motto 'A happy holly and a merry berry' on the wall of a lavatory.

But wassails are only one of the many kinds of song sung then, which still survive now. The proof is in the retention of subject matter. The carols to the Boar's Head must stem from that time, for 'the Boar's Head was the favoured dish in the great Yule festival of the Northmen' (Chambers' *Encyclopaedia*). Carols with sacred trees as subject are survivals from the Germano-Celtic Yule rites, for the mistletoe we all remember, and the holly and the ivy were a pair almost as sacred. It is not only in carol and song that the power of trees survives today. Girls are still named Hazel in honour of that first, fruitful tree (as they are still named Ivy, of course).

Any carol that refers to May or spring must undoubtedly have a pagan origin, as Christianity has no festival for either. 'As it fell out one May morning. On the bright holiday' is straight from the folk-song of the past. In general, any subject which is not in the Bible is from the folk, and the folk were pagan, as we shall see.

People still knew the cause of their celebrations till about 1600. That was when carols lost their popularity, and printed ones swiftly disappeared. A map of London in Elizabethan times shows every church with a cock on the steeple. He still stands on many. But, till then, people knew why he was there. Now, he's for the weather.

One of the most striking evidences of pagan survival is provided by Professor Geoffrey Webb, Secretary of the Royal Commission on Historical Monuments. He had been assigned to the survey of those ancient churches which had suffered damage in the 1939–45 war, and he found that ninety per cent of all churches built before 1350 had a stone phallus concealed within the altar.* Till 1350 the generative principle was worshipped. That is why there was so much greenery carved on pillars and screens—amongst it, the Green Man, with stems coming out of his mouth; why there were the folk-carvings on misericords; why there were the realistic representations of women with open legs; why beasts and masks, symbolic of reproduction, were put as 'gargoyles' outside the building. It is because of the generative principle that people are still married, baptized and ultimately buried in church.

Paganism survived strongly in England till about 1600, and it survives today, in all our customs, all our folk-values, but unrecognized. Yet the time from 1350

* From 'The Roots of Witchcraft' by Michael Harrison, Tandem Books. On page 215 it is stated that Professor Webb's discoveries are fully supported by photographs.

to 1550 is 'the golden age of the English Carol' according to the *Encyclopaedia Britannica.* That, of course, was when many of the Yule-tide carols were converted. That was when Yule became Christ's Mass.

Together with some contemporary love-songs, the carols were then written down, with their new gloss of doctrine. But the date of recording (mis-recording) must not be confused with the date of composition. 'The Holly and the Ivy' was first recorded in 1710. Does anyone suppose it was composed then?

Between 1350 and 1550 there were no pious peasants, overwhelmed with the purity of the Virgin Mary, to compose Christmas carols. There were peasants overjoyed with the fertility of Mother Earth and Mother Eve, celebrating them with songs and dances which shocked every ascetic priest in every village.

It is on written record. There were twenty-two denunciations of folk-song and dance as sin in the Middle Ages (Greene, *The Early English Carols*). In one of them, the folk's songs at festivals were described as '*obscenus, turpis, luxuriosus, indecens, diabolicus*'— 'obscene, shameful, wanton, indecent, devilish'. It doesn't seem the Church found them pious.

Dancing was worse. Yet a carol is a dance-song. The leader of the dance was often a woman, 'The bellcow of a herd with the devil for master' (Greene). What Greene does not tell is that the woman might be naked: there is a sixteenth-century carving of morris dancers in Lancaster Museum which shows a naked girl leading them. Beneath it is a modern text saying she was probably a boy disguised.

People were dancing inside the churches until at least 1338—that was when it was forbidden in Wells Cathedral. Outside the church, in the churchyards, it went on till the sixteenth century. Why? Why did people ever dance in church? Why not on the village green? Because the ancestors are buried in and around the church, and they need to take a watching part in the mating of the young. Our church was like the men's sacred house ('temple') in New Guinea, with the ancestors' skulls up in the roof, and the Tree of Life painted over the door.

The word 'carol' still meant sin in the fifteenth century. In 1497 a monk wrote, 'And ever his house was void of Carols and dissolute songs.' Birds of a feather . . . What were ordinary folk's houses full of? Another wrote, 'At Christmas, flee and hide from the dishonest, shameful songs which excite lust and lead to shameful imaginings which are hard to expel' (Greene).

What kind of carol were they writing about? There are rare survivals. Two lines, only, from the thirteenth century were preserved in a monk's sermon:

At wrestling my lover I choose,
And at stone-casting to him I lose.

He allegorized them into some approximate Christian moralizing, the stone casting became the fighting for the hard (stony) hearts of men and women, and the wrestling was the fight for eternal bliss.

There is a whole song from two centuries later:

She was a maid with a *sun-burnt* arse   [brenten]
She rode to mill upon a horse,
Yet she was *made-en* ne'er the worse.   [mayden]

Chorus:
Sing dillum, dillum, dill,
I can tell you, and I will
Of my *darling's* water-mill.   [ladyes]

Then laid she was upon a sack,
'Strike soft' she said 'hurt not my back,
But spare not; make the old mill clack.'

I'm sure the miller was full nice,
His millstones both hung by a vice,
And they were *rolling* in a trice.   [Walkynge]

This maid to mill did oft resort,
But of her *sport* made no report,   [game]
Yet 'twas to her full great comfort.*

It is rare to find such an unaltered carol, because all
the recorders were clerics, the clerks in holy orders.
Some of those, in the beginning, would have been
pagan priests who managed to reconcile themselves
to Christian beliefs. But by the fifteenth century the
priesthood had learnt its new doctrine. 'Nearly all of
the written songs have a religious or didactic character,' says Greene. But the folk-songs themselves were
still *'obscenus, turpis* etc'. So nearly all of these written
carols were written down by proper monks. We have
to analyse their writings and use knowledge from
secular sources. We can scarcely hope to find new
manuscripts, by a pagan priest who had learned to
write. Who would have preserved them? Who would
have preserved him? Was Rabelais the one who got
away?

But some folk were still pagan in 1350, 1550 and
later, for dancing round the maypole was still going on
when the Puritans came to power in 1650. They forbade
it, because they knew its origin and meaning—that the
pole was a phallic symbol, decorated with flowers,
danced round for the spring celebrations. At dawn, the
people went to gather the May flowers, with their

*(No. 460, *The Early English Carols*; original words at text-side)

129

peculiar scent of semen, and 'many a green gown was given'. Greene says about the original May carols: 'The May festival celebrated freedom in love, and heaped abuse upon husbands and faithfulness in marriage.' With the restoration of Charles II, the maypoles were erected again, some taller than ever!

As always, the customs, the attitudes still live, now. This year, next year, people at Padstow will sing:

Unite, and unite, and let us all unite,
For Summer is a-coming today,
And whither we are going, there we will all unite,
In the merry morning of May.

They don't mean 'Let us join a Trade Union.' They do mean that once there was a time when the whole community took part in a social and celebratory love-making.

In England pagan May customs and New Year customs, and all the other customs, do survive, but obscured or repressed. The overt ones, the mummers, the morris dancers, the songs like 'John Barleycorn' are a small minority and survive hardly. But in Scotland pagan customs survive hardily! There, first-footers, whisky-drinkers, 'Should auld acquaintance be forgot' are the overwhelming majority! Hogmanay is still the word. The Scots still could not, and would not, produce a Christmas folk-song. I don't doubt that a Presbyterian minister could produce a Christmas hymn, but how would he get it sung?

Of course he'd go for television, and some Christian pop-singer like Cliff Richard. But in the fifteenth century church-attenders were the mass audience, the church choirs the recording artists. So the second set of missionaries that came to England answered the question in their contemporary manner.

The first set—those who arrived in England from

Rome in 597—seem to have done nothing about the carols at all. They'd converted the kings, and the kings had converted the people by royal decree. It was a simple method but had its defects. Now came the friars, the Franciscan friars especially, in 1224. They were more numerous, more powerful, than their predecessors. They were to convert the people—and get paid for it.

We, today, have a preconception of the poverty and goodness of Franciscan friars. But then they were the begging friars, on the streets, in the houses, begging in a more direct way than they do now. They found the carols very suitable for their double aim—propaganda and money. Popular tunes would draw the crowd, the adapted words would penetrate the minds, and the atmosphere of good fellowship would encourage giving. This is how a contemporary saw the friars in action:

He was an easy man in penance giving
Where he could hope to make a decent living:
It's a sure sign wherever gifts are given
To a poor Order that a man's well shriven,
And should he give enough, he knew in verity
The penitent repented in sincerity . . .
He kept his tippet stuffed with pins for curls,
And pocket-knives to give to pretty girls.
And certainly his voice was gay and sturdy,
For he sang well and played the hurdy-gurdy.
At sing-songs he was champion of the hour.*

He played the hurdy-gurdy. The Salvation Army play the tambourine. Pop-singers play the guitar.

We do know the name of the Franciscan friar who wrote one quarter of all the carols recorded between 1350 and 1550. He wrote 166 songs in all, 119 of them

*(*Chaucer, In Modern English,* by Nevill Coghill)

in carol form. He is Friar Ryman. At sing-songs he, too, must have been champion of the hour! With such an output, he might be a good poet—another Burns! An examination of his work shows, however, that, 'He used Latin, and several times composed a series of Carols in the same strain and using the same Burden (Chorus), either in identical form, or slight variations . . . Ryman is to be regarded as a conscientious, rather uninspired Franciscan' (Greene). Even the 'conscientious' must be politeness. The examiner did not wish to mark his work too severely.

The best example is the worst. Here is the best-worst example of a carol's conversion I have found.

Here comes Holly that is so *gent;*   [gentle]
To please all men is his intent.
Alleluia

Chorus:
Alleluia, Alleluia,
Alleluia now sing we.

But, lord and lady of this hall
Whoever against Holly call,
Alleluia

Whoever against Holly do cry
In a lepe* shall be hang full high.
Allelulia

Whoever against Holly do sing,
He may weep and his hands wring,
Allelulia.

---

* 'Lepe' is translated 'basket' by the Rev. Routley, who quotes the carol. But it suggests 'loop' to me, and so 'noose'.

That one-word addition of 'Alleluia' is called 'magnificently irrelevant' by Routley. We can agree on its irrelevance.

But it is revelatory of the method of a converting friar. He keeps some, and he adds some. Now it is here that I disagree with Greene, from whose book I have taken much information and with whose judgement I often agree. For Greene thinks that, 'The Carols were composed on the model of secular pieces which they hoped to displace.' But there is no thorough re-modelling here, only slap-dash addition. Greene goes on: 'They were not popular by origin, but by destination'. I think they were popular by origin, because of all the folk parts they retain. It is the bad joining of those with the Christian doctrine which makes 'magnificent irrelevance' in the Carols we shall examine.

Estimations of the merit of the remodelling, the rewriting, will vary. What cannot be varied is the fact of rewriting. There is documentary proof of the original pagan (or secular) carol existing side by side with the priest's rewriting of it. One can only wonder why it hasn't been destroyed. There exists still the Red Book of Ossory, now in the Bishop's Palace of Kilkenny, which has sixty songs composed by the Franciscan Bishop of Ossory. Above sixteen of them are written some of the original words. 'Doo, doo, nightingale, Sing well, merrily, Shall I never for thy Love longer care' is written above *'Regem adoremus, Superne curie, Matri jubilemus, Regine glorie.'* 'Let us worship the King, O supreme guardian. Let us rejoice in the Mother, O glorious Queen.' A different God needs different words—but is jealous of the tunes. Unfortunately, the bishop didn't write down all the original he was working from. His Preface is as unwise as the statement made by someone charged with an offence by the police: 'Be advised, reader, that the Bishop of Ossory has made these songs for the vicars of the cathedral church, for the priests and for his clerks, to be sung on the important holidays and at celebrations, in order that their throats and mouths consecrated to God, may not be polluted by songs which are lewd, secular, and associated with revelry.' He's admitting that the priests and the clerks had been singing the others. The priests must have come from peasant families.

Later, in the seventeenth century, exactly the same thing was done. Another Franciscan bishop, Luke Wadding, took the tunes of songs he named as 'Fortune my foe' and 'I do not love cause thou art fair' for his 'A Pious Garland'.

I would not like the reader to think that the process stopped then or was practised only by the Franciscans. In 1696 Nahum Tate took a folk-tune and wrote 'While Shepherds Watched' to it. As far as I know, the folk-words were obliterated. In 1825 the Religious Tract Society published a version of 'God Rest You Merry, Gentlemen' with the 'merry' left out. The Society for the Propagation of Christian Knowledge published, in 1831, a book of 'Christmas carols' which were all hymns. In 1853 the Reverend Neale changed 'The Spring Carol', which he found in *'Piae Cantones'*, into 'Good King Wenceslas'. Bishop Phillips Brooks, in 1900, wrote 'O little Town of Bethlehem' to a folk-tune. (He behaved like a real pagan—he got up to see the sun rise over Bethlehem.) Abroad, in Germany, 'It was Luther and the Protestants who were the great rewriters of Carols' (Greene).

The truth is, all Christians everywhere in Germany, France, Spain, Africa, the South Seas, prefer hymns to native carols. Accordingly, all over the world, carols have been converted. A fertility religion has met a sterility religion. 'Take these Gospels. They'll give you sins. I can cure those.'

Forms have been partially kept but meaning wholly

changed. 'The English religious Carol, far from being the product of the popular joy at the Christmas season, is one weapon of the Church in her long struggle against paganism' (Greene). It is a struggle which will be won when no more children are born.

Some of the Churchmen's names, who have waged that struggle in the past, are known. But 'Without doubt, more of the friars' number than have left any written trace, both composed and sang many Carols like those ... collected' (Greene). Those unknown friars taught the peasants' children to sing them, and later their children's children's children sang them to folk-song collectors, and they became the traditional carols that have no manuscript record. Oh simple faith of the folk-song collectors! How nice that the old songs have no sex in them, not like these modern songs!

An indoctrinator not only changes the message. He also changes the tone, because he has a different relationship with the singers. He is a man set apart, not one of them. So, suddenly, 'we' become 'you'. Someone tells us what to do:

Now like the snake your skin
Cast off, of evil thoughts and sin.

We are known! We are commanded! This cannot be a folk-song. Who thought of people as sinners? Who said to others 'Therefore repent'?*

An ascetic is not happy with the world and the flesh. That's why he adds 'and the devil' to them. So, wherever we find grief instead of joy, we see the black hand. Suddenly, there is no celebration, no 'Merry Christmas!' Lines are added about the Crucifixion (at Easter!) to a Christmas carol. There wasn't enough unhappiness in Christ's birth, for a rejector of birth.

* From No. 42, 'Remember' *Oxford Book of Carols.*

His head they crowned with thorn,
And at him they did laugh and scorn,
Who for our good was born;
God send us a happy New Year!

(From 'The Greensleeves Carol')

That 'New Year' gives it all away, gives the monk away, adding his three black lines on top of it. He must have found 'Happy New Year!' stick in his throat every time he said it.

Adding in doctrine, adding in Bible story—and especially adding them in hastily—will disrupt the sense, the lines and the rhymes. The reader may have noticed the broken word-order of the lines about casting off your skin like the snake. As a rule, any break in the sense is a sign of the breaking and entering of the thief. People did not, in 1350 to 1550, compose and sing nonsense. Someone did, who didn't care if one portion was left nonsensical as long as his portion made sense. There were no simple peasants. There were priests simple enough to believe that, because no one dared question their work in the Middle Ages, no one would dare later on.

The effect of combining carol with doctrine was to kill most of the carols. They couldn't take it. Shall we say, the people wouldn't take it? Only four of Greene's collection of nearly five hundred were found still being sung as folk-songs. Of the seventy traditional carols in the *Oxford Book of Carols,* I had heard about ten sung. Of course, some more regular church-goer may have heard more—but not sung by the folk. It is a proof that words do matter. The bad words killed the good tunes. No matter how good the tune, no one will sing:

The next good joy that Mary had
It was the joy of six
To see her own son Jesus Christ
Upon the crucifix.
(From 'Joys Seven')

The editor of the OBC has taken it upon himself to remove from the carols all the verses which accused the Jews. Quite right. But who wrote them? His example shows that, as soon as people are free to think, they reject what they think wrong.

To that conscious objection must be added the unconscious rejection of poor poetry. Many believers, singers of the Christian carols without an objection in their heads, find they cannot remember all the words. Hence the printed carol sheets at the Christmas services. Children, going carol-singing, never know all the verses. They know the beginning only—because that is the original, meaningful part. After that, they rush to 'We wish you a merry Christmas, We wish you a merry Christmas' and ring the door-bell, not only because they want the money quickly but because they cannot remember the story whose thread has been broken by doctrine.

Of course the hasty mixture is defended by Churchmen today. What else can they do? It's too late to revise it. So, some Apocryphal gospel is found, some 'legend' which is near enough to the original song to make a cover-story. The Reverend Routley explains 'I Saw Three Ships' thus: 'The legend, behind it, is connected with the Magi . . . The tradition was that their remains were brought to Byzantium by the Empress Helena . . . and later taken to Milan. From Milan, the skulls of the Three Kings were taken to Cologne by Frederick Barbarossa in 1162, and are believed to be still preserved as relics in the cathedral there. The "three ships" are traditionally the ships by which they were brought to Cologne. The Carol has simply transferred the ships from the Magi to Christ himself.' Is that an explanation or an obscuration? 'Simply' does it.

Cecil Sharp, who often went round collecting songs with the local vicar, writes in *The English Carol:* 'The rustic's simplicity disarms criticism, just as his pious, intense, child-like belief in every detail of the Gospel narrative banishes scepticism.' Alas no. My scepticism found itself much needed in England. My criticism, as well armed as I can equip it, points out that many of the details so piously, intensely and childishly believed in, are not in any Gospel at all! Where were the rustics to trace the tradition of the three ships or of the 'Joys Seven'? Especially when they couldn't read. 'The Carols are the work of all the people combined' writes the Reverend Percy Dearmer, editor of the *Oxford Book of Carols.* And so they are. For the people composed them, the priests altered them, and the gentry enforced them.

How can the carols be restored? We have the retained subject-matter, our knowledge of the customs, and our understanding of the symbolism, to help us. Having removed the over-writing, we see the subject-matter of the original and can compare it with similar songs which did escape. For all these carols are folk-songs which follow a type. We are not dealing with a song-writer's lyric creations. So, we are able to foretell how the old carols would have continued.

Now, if we discard completely the over-writing, the Christianity, we shall miss vital clues. For the over-writing has been suggested by what was there. It is rarely completely new. Usually, the nearest parallel has been adopted. Any woman can become the Virgin Mary. Winter changes into Satan and sin. The priests were not trying to do a good job, just a quick one, like a carpenter with putty.

Our guide is also the form of the carol. First, the

rhymes. Rhymes are hard for a Ryman. Puns are too easy for me. Any rough-and-ready restorer will try to retain the received rhymes and (alliteration!) 'Keep the rhyme and bodge the sense' is the working practice of hedge-carpenters! The example which forces itself forward is:

Now the holly he bears a berry as white as the milk;
And Mary bore Jesus who was wrapped up in silk.*

The 'Mary bore Jesus' was the priest's essential addition. After that, all he wanted was a rhyme. Now, my rhyming dictionary gives only two other possibilities—'bilk' and 'ilk'. So he couldn't find another and had to keep to the original 'silk', though it's obviously wrong. Jesus in silk? Well, people have gone on singing it. They've got used to all hymns being nonsense. But that rhyme-word points the sense, as does our knowledge of holly-symbolism, and our thought that holly demands a response from ivy.

Every carol, every song, has its pattern. The art is to keep it. So where it's not kept is where the doctrine is inserted. The beginning is usually retained unaltered. 'I Saw Three Ships' begins with question and answer. Then come the 'rejoicing' verses that do not follow the pattern. They are the insert, the doctoring.

No wonder the later indoctrinators, more apprehensive of criticism, scrapped all the words and kept the tune only. But even that is trying to help us. It used to fit the words, and the tone of the words. It does not fit the hasty emendations, even when these emendations scan and rhyme. 'Good King Wenceslas' does scan and rhyme. But the tune it took over was for the 'Flower Carol'. So, there is an oddity about singing 'When the snow lay round about/Deep and crisp and even' to a tune meant for 'Life in all her growing

*(From 'The Holly Bears a Berry')

powers/Towards the light is striving.' The oddity is more stressed when the dance-rhythm can be heard beneath a Christianized song. It is certain that there was a unity between celebration, words and tune. The right words will fit perfectly, and people will want to sing them. The carols' popularity in the future should equal their popularity in the past.

The degree of accuracy of any restoration from all these pointers, varies. But the fact that there is some guidance for all of them means that they are never personal versions. Generally, where there is much of the pagan original, the restoration is well directed. Where there has been much rewriting, and less of the original survives, the restoration is less well aimed. But where there is only one sign of a pagan original, any attempt to restore the whole will be an improvement, will be better than leaving it perverted. A traditional Christian carol is a contradiction in terms.

By restoring these carols, I have shown that some part of a Christian festival has been adapted from an earlier pagan one. If that part, why not others? Where have the church's prayers come from? The benedictions? The responses? Where have the services of baptism, marriage and burial their origin? Where did the Mass come from? Possibly all could be restored.

The old Nature festivals are popular still; and, with the ceremonies of birth, marriage and death are the most wanted of the Church's services. They are the most popular precisely because they are the most pagan. Christianity is the slowly dying graft, which has not taken. The Christian carols are the cut flowers of paganism.

The restoration of the true carols is the restoration of meaning, of sense and of a happy outlook. The black priests have been caught stealing the flowery vestments of their predecessors. The 'unconquerability' of Man is celebrated, not his weakness and his sinfulness.

The re-writing of history has been righted!

If people like the restored understanding of the link between themselves and Nature, and the community spirit that makes any celebration possible, a different society will have to be created to fit their liking. The carols did, in one sense, come from a 'golden age', an age without sexual repression. The age that sings them again will be one that acknowledges sexual love as the supreme experience—puts the cock back on the steeple—and celebrates the turning-points of Nature and Man's nature, his spring, his summer, his autumn, even his winter. If you light a sparkler this Yule, and write 'To the Unconquered Sun' in the air with it, you will begin.

Humanists can join neo-pagans in these carols. There is no reason why they should not, and every feeling why they should. We shall all join a world-wide, non-doctrinal folk-philosophy and connect ourselves with the past.

Africans say 'A man is but a link between his ancestors and his descendants.' The link is also language.

ACKNOWLEDGEMENTS:

I owe a great deal to the Introduction to *The Early English Carols,* by R. L. Greene, published by the Oxford University Press. From it I gained the knowledge of the work of the Franciscan friars and of the long struggle between folk-paganism and the Church. It provides a foundation for my own work of criticism of the carol texts. I used the first edition, but there is now a second edition, with a slightly altered Introduction. Here I have restored some of the carols he so carefully recorded.

The current versions of the others are from The *Oxford University Press Book of Carols.*

Holly and Ivy
Carols

The Holly and the Ivy
(Current version)

The holly and the ivy,
When they are both full grown,
Of all the trees that are in the wood,
The holly bears the crown.

Chorus:
The rising of the sun,
And the running of the deer,
The playing of the merry organ,
Sweet singing in the choir.

The holly bears a blossom
As white as the lily flower,
And Mary bore sweet Jesus Christ
To be our sweet Saviour.

The holly bears a berry
As red as any blood,
And Mary bore sweet Jesus Christ
To do poor sinners good.

The holly bears a prickle
As sharp as any thorn,
And Mary bore sweet Jesus Christ
On Christmas Day in the morn.

The holly bears a bark
As bitter as any gall,
And Mary bore sweet Jesus Christ
For to redeem us all.

The holly and the ivy
When they are both full grown,
Of all the trees that are in the wood,
The holly bears the crown.

The great pair! Let me speak for them. We still associate them, wreathe them together. They are both evergreens, but the holly and the ivy are evergreen in more than one sense. They are Man and Woman, going on for ever.

I wish to make their symbolism live again. In so doing, I shall restore the original, pagan carol, the dance-song that used the symbolism meaningfully, for the Christmas carol destroyed the meaning by substituting a hymn for half of it.

First, the holly tree needs looking at, for the basis of all symbolism is a link between appearance (or deed) and some other thing it resembles. The clumps of red berries are the scarlet, male colour. Their shape is phallic. The leaves have prickles. So the fruit and foliage become symbols of maleness.

The 'deed' the tree does is to bear its berries at the worst time of the year. It overcomes the dark and cold of winter, exactly as the Unconquered Sun does. It makes its boast in the face of its enemies like an Anglo-Saxon warrior! So the holly is a symbol of a fruitful warrior-hero.

Ivy, too, bears her buds in winter. Women are still called Ivy. The tree's appearance and way of growth are traditionally feminine—'Just like the ivy, I'll cling to you.' The smooth leaf, the whitish vine, suggest smooth skin and white body.

This traditional symbolism has, in modern times, sunk to the subconscious level. But several of *The Early English Carols* show it being consciously used and folklorists still know of it. 'A berried holly is a sacred tree which seems to belong to a male cult. The

144

Holly Boy and the Ivy Girl are still spoken of at Christmas time' (Ruth Tongue, *Somerset Folklore*). The editor of *The Oxford Book of Carols* (*OBC*) writes: 'The subject is probably of pagan origin, and symbolised the masculine (holly) and the feminine (ivy) elements.'

So now we know what the folk were singing about. The very next line fixes the time—'When they are both full grown'—when lad and girl are mature. The earliest version gave 'Now are both well grown' to emphasize the present time of the singing and the dancing—these present young men and women. The last line of the first verse—'The holly bears the crown' tells us why they are singing. Man is king.

It's a question of who is dominant. 'In some old English Carols, holly and ivy are put into a curious antagonism, apparently connected with a contest of the sexes' (Clement Miles, *Christmas in Ritual and Tradition*).

In that contest, the women will not sing 'The holly bears the crown.' They have been left out by the Christian rewriter. He did not want a contest of the sexes, or anything sexual, and began his changes here, at the end of the first verse. But, by retaining only what the men sang, he has made a grammatical error. The opening subject is plural—the holly and the ivy— but the verb 'bears' is singular. By deduction, the women sang, 'The ivy bears the crown.' If we picture the two rings of young men and women, the one singing while the other danced round, we can see the men singing first, then the girls repeating the first verse but changing the last line. The challenges have been made. The Christian explanation is that Jesus, wore a crown of holly at the crucifixion. That's a different challenge.

Verses 2, 3 and 4 are all broken in half. The first two lines are the men's claim. The second two are the

145

Church's claim, the added doctrine. How badly the two fit! That poor word 'and'! It has to try to join the holly's bearing of blossom, berry, prickle, bark, with Mary's bearing a son. Tree and woman don't match. Tree and tree, or man and woman, those are the right pairings. Also, the holly's bearing is changing, progressing, while Mary's bearing stays the same. The parallel is not being followed. 'Sweet Jesus Christ' is repeated four times. There is no narrative or doctrinal change to match the tree's change.

Further, there is grammatical error again. The holly 'bears'. Mary 'bore'. The rewriter is having to compare not only a tree with a woman but a living tree with a dead woman.

If we take out the second parts of the verses, what remains?

The holly bears a blossom,
As white as the lily flower.
The holly bears a berry
As red as any blood.
The holly bears a prickle
As sharp as any thorn.
The holly bears a bark
As bitter as any gall.

Why are those parts of the tree given, in that order? Because they follow 'The holly bears the crown.' These are the male attributes, attempting to show that man is king. They are all symbolic. For, if the holly's real development were being realistically described, the order would be bark, prickle, flower, berry. Certainly berry would come at the end. But the bark, the bitter bark, is here the conclusion, and prickle comes after berry. So a metaphor between holly tree and man is being developed. These half-verses are telling symbolically, of masculine changes, from

146

white blossom to red berry, to sharp prickle and the bitterness that prickle can bring.

The difficulty of conveying that meaning in the image of the tree's growth accounts for two failures to keep up the parallels. A holly tree has berries. But man has only one berry. So the tree is forced to bear one, only, because the underlying meaning in any symbol is the important one.

Any symbolic poem succeeds in so far as the underlying comparison fits the realistic appearance. But this relationship is hard to sustain—indeed, impossible, for one thing is not another—and sometimes the appearance has to be forced to fit. Here, the holly's blossom is 'as white as the lily flower'. In fact, it's a greenish white. Man's singular blossom, before it is a berry, is white through under-exposure.

We have no meaningless list. Holly is declaring his powers and, by concluding with the bitterness he can leave, is in bitter contest with Ivy. Where has she gone? She has gone from the place which the Church took from her. She was in all the second halves of the verse, making her counter claim to bear the crown. Each second half should begin 'And ivy bears', so matching tree to tree, tense to tense. The same symbolism of sexual growth, sexual power, would be followed. Her answer—the girls' answer—would outdo the young men's claim, so that they have to increase its strength each time. Otherwise the song could not progress. The girls' last retort must be to that bitterness, a reply that makes a conclusion to the rivalry.

The chorus is divided as the verses are. The first two lines are the male symbolism of the sun rising and of deer-chasing. Ivy's response, in place of the church organ and choir, must be with her symbols—the moon waxing, and the deer catching the hunter! For deer-chasing is ivy-plucking.

The last verse, as well as making a satisfying conclusion to the rivalry (the dance can't end in a fight), must be like the first verse, so like it, that the Christian adapter thought the repetition would be adequate. It must answer the question 'Who bears the crown?' The answer, in life, is that men and women must bear one together. In symbolism, it is that the holly and ivy wreath is man and woman's love. When it is taken to the grave of relatives at New Year, the round wreath is a sign that love goes on, that the family goes on. Mortuary customs are among those we have inherited from our German and Celtic ancestors, according to the *Encyclopaedia Britannica.*

The Holly and the Ivy
(Restored)

1.   *Men:*   The holly and the ivy,
                 When they are both full-grown,
                 Of all the trees that are in the wood,
                 The holly bears the crown.

    Women: The holly and the ivy,
                 When they are both full-grown,
                 Of all the trees that are in the wood,
                 The ivy bears the crown.

    Men: The rising of the sun,
                 And the running of the deer:
    Women: The rounding of the shining moon,
                 The weary, worn hunter.

2.   *Men:*   The holly bears a blossom
                 As white as the lily-flower:
    Women: And ivy bears the blackest buds
                 To pull him to her power.

	Men:	The rising of the sun,
		And the running of the deer:
	Women:	The rounding of the shining moon,
		The weary, worn hunter.

3.   *Men:*   The holly bears a berry
               As red as any blood:
   Women: And ivy bears the greenest leaves
               To wrap him in her hood.

   Men: The rising of the sun,
               And the running of the deer:
   Women: The rounding of the shining moon,
               The weary, worn hunter.

4.   *Men:*   The holly bears a prickle
               As sharp as any thorn:
   Women: And ivy bears a clinging vine
               To smother him right down.

   Men: The rising of the sun,
               And the running of the deer:
   Women: The rounding of the shining moon,
               The weary, worn hunter.

5.   *Men:*   The holly bears a bark
               As bitter as any gall:
   Women: And ivy bears small, nectar flowers
   (slower): To sweeten all his fall.

6.   *Men and* The holly and the ivy,
   Women: When they are both full-grown,
               Of all the trees that are in the wood
               These two will wreathe as one.

The Early English Carols
No. 138 (Modernized English)

Chorus:
Ivy, chief of trees it is,
Veni, coronaberis. [Come, you shall be crowned].
The most worthy she is in town,
He that sayeth other doth amiss,
And worthy to bear the crown;
Veni, coronaberis.

Ivy is soft and meek of speech;
Against all trouble she is bliss;
Well is he that may her reach;
Veni, coronaberis.

Ivy is green with colour bright;
Of all trees best she is;
And that I prove well now be right;
Veni, coronaberis.

Ivy beareth berries black;
God grant us all his bliss;
For there we shall nothing lack;
Veni, coronaberis.

Ivy is the chief of trees because it is woman. That's why a tree can be 'soft and meek of speech'. Ivy is 'worthy to bear the crown' because she is worthy of being sovereign—queen. As in 'The Holly and the Ivy', this rivalry between man's tree, holly, and woman's tree, ivy, underlies the song. It's the old pagan symbolism—holly, ivy, mistletoe, hazel, oak—back to the sacred grove.

This pagan, sexual song was written down by a priest—the only clerks were clerics. He couldn't tolerate some parts of it. So he put in Latin instead, and just one line about God. Let's look at that.

Ivy beareth berries black
God grant us all his bliss
For there we shall nothing lack.

It doesn't join at either end. The priest is like a kid who can't use a ruler. He's rubbed something out and can't join it up again neatly. It doesn't join 'berries black', and God isn't 'there'. So God grant us our second line back!

Who are 'we'? We are holly, every man of us. Where we men shall nothing lack is where Ivy bears berries black. Where woman bears berries black. Where? On her breasts. Before I realized that, I too had been reading words on a page. No wonder the priest did a bit of hasty over-writing!

And then comes his Latin, his '*Veni coronaberis*', in every chorus. I wonder if he ever thought that people who weren't priests would be able to understand Latin and that some of them would be critical, openly. I guess he couldn't see so far ahead. For 'Come, you shall be crowned' is another *non sequitur*. It won't join on 'And worthy to bear the crown', in the first verse. It will just repeat it. In fact, that's what he's done—taken that sense, though he doesn't want trees crowned, it's too pagan. And he took that sense and put it in Latin, because '*coronaberis*' kept the rhyme. It's got 'berries' in. He took the suggested word that kept the rhyme and so gives away the sense of the line he tried to re-write: 'Come, with your berries.'

The whole song is in praise of woman, of her many qualities, her softness of speech and of her evergreenness but above all, of her berries. 'Well is he that may her reach.' Touch. 'And that I prove well now be right.'

He isn't proving colour just by seeing. He's proving by proof.

My first restoration followed the original rhyme-scheme. But I needed a tune. And I found 'To be a Pilgrim' longing to get away from Bunyan. Vaughan Williams had arranged a marriage between the two in 1906. Before that, the tune was a folk-tune titled 'Our Captain Calls'. So I freed it for the folk again. It preferred 'To be a pagan' and it prefers a new rhyme-scheme.

The 'Best of Trees' Carol (Restored: Tune: 'To Be A Pilgrim')

Solo:	Ivy is the best of trees,
Chorus:	Come, bear thy berries.
Solo:	She's the tree that doth men please,
Chorus:	Come, bear thy berries.
Solo:	She's worth more than all the town,
	Gold, jewels, or king's crown,
	Still more, without a gown,
Chorus:	Come, bear thy berries.

Solo:	Ivy is the best of trees,
Chorus:	Come, bear thy berries.
Solo:	She's the tree that doth men please,
Chorus:	Come, bear thy berries.
Solo:	She is kind and soft of speech,
	Love's language she doth teach,
	To him, who can them reach,
Chorus:	Come, bear thy berries.

Solo:	Ivy is the best of trees,
Chorus:	Come, bear thy berries.
Solo:	She's the tree that doth men please,
Chorus:	Come, bear thy berries.

Solo:	Evergreen, and always young,
	Smooth joys are round her hung,
	I'd prove what I have sung,
Chorus:	Come, bear thy berries.
Solo:	Ivy is the best of trees,
Chorus:	Come, bear thy berries.
Solo:	She's the tree that doth men please,
Chorus:	Come, bear thy berries.
Solo:	She has berries brown or black,
	They show where there's no lack,
	Bear them, and hold not back,
Chorus:	Come, bear thy berries.

The Early English Carols

No. 136 (Modernized English)

Chorus:
Nay, Ivy, nay, it shall not be, certainly;
Let Holly have the mastery as the manner is.

Holly and his merry men, they dance and they sing;
Ivy and her maidens, they weep and they *wring*.
[suffer: wring their hands]

Ivy has a chilblain; she caught it with the cold;
So must all they, always, that with Ivy hold.

Holly has berries as red as any rose,
The forester, the hunter, keep them from the does.

Ivy has berries as black as any sloes,
There comes the *wolf** and eats them as he goes.

Holly has birds, a full, fair flock,
The nightingale, the popinjay, the gentle laverock.

Good Ivy, what birds have you?
None but the owlet, that cries 'How! How!'

Note: I have omitted the first verse as I do not use it in my restoration. It is 'Holly stands in the hall, fair to behold. Ivy stands outside the door, she is sorely cold.'

Not 'Ivy is the best of trees', but 'Holly is the master-tree'. Young men are taking up the challenge the women have already sung. It does look as if the

*Oule in the manuscript, but it can't be right: it's a woman symbol. Was our cleric copying 'woulf'?

sex-war is an unpleasant form of flirting. Except for the last verse. That redeems the tone with a touch of humour.

And I don't find the song really unpleasant, because it can't be taken seriously. Fancy saying that young men keep their berries from young women! They will, until the young women think they're old enough. Then we'll see who's cold. The young men's lack of confidence, beneath all that bragging, is still in the old song. 'Let holly have the mastery.' Please!

I like the way men and women are linked with trees and birds. Holly, nightingales, popinjays and laverocks are all male symbols; and ivy, does, sloes and owlets are all female. Seeing likenesses to ourselves in trees and animals makes us like those trees and animals. Men used to plant a holly by their front door. Ivy leaves were a favourite decoration on jugs and cups.

There are two reasons why the Carol isn't still sung, isn't still as well known as 'The Holly and the Ivy'. First, the point got lost. People, now, don't understand 'Good ivy, what birds have you? None but the owlet that cries "How! How!" ' We've lost the power of seeing likeness. The owlet is in the woods at night. That's where young girls are given cause to cry 'Ooo! Ooo!' or even 'How? How?'

A wise old owl lived in an oak;
The more she saw the less she spoke;
The less she spoke, the more she saw.
So would you, if you held your jaw.

There's a nursery rhyme 'Restored To Its Adult Original'. And—second reason—the tune got lost, got taken. Words without tunes never to hearts go. None of *The Early English Carols* have tunes. Clerics are words-men not tunes-men.

Luckily, I found a tunes-woman. Yes, a woman.

The Young Men's Carol (Restored)

Solo Man: Our holly and men, we dance and we sin
Your ivy and maids, you weep and you cl
Your ivy feels chill, she droops in the col
So must all you women that with her hol

Chorus, Men: No, ivy, no, you shall not change the rule
Let holly have mast'ry as usual.

Solo Man: Our holly has berries, as red as the rose,
Strong for'ster, young hunter, keep
them from the does.
Your ivy has berries, as black as the sloe:
But wide roves our wolf and he gulps
as he goes.

Chorus, Men: No, ivy, no, you shall not change the rule
Let holly have mast'ry as usual.

Solo Man.   Our holly has birds, a great, handsome f
The nightingale, peacock, the uprising l
Poor ivy! poor ivy! what birds go with yo
The night owl that cries out 'Oo! Oo! Oo!

Chorus, Men: No, ivy, no, you shall not change the rule
Let holly have mast'ry as usual.

Young Men's Carol

Music © 1984 Gloria Newton

SOLO Our | hol-ly and men, we | dance and we sing. Your | i-vy and maids, you

weep and you cling. Your | i-vy feels chill, she | droops in the cold. So

must all you wo-men that | with her hold | No, I— vy no, | you shall

not change the rule, | Let | hol-ly have mast-'ry os | us — u- al

157

The Sans Day Carol

(Current Version)

Solo: Now the holly bears a berry as white as the milk
           And Mary bore Jesus who was wrapped up in si.
Chorus: And Mary bore Jesus our Saviour for to be,
           And the first tree in the green wood
           It was the holly, holly, holly,
           And the first tree in the green wood
           It was the holly!

Solo: Now the holly bears a berry as green as the gras
           And Mary bore Jesus who died on the cross.

Chorus: And Mary bore Jesus our Saviour for to be,
           And the first tree in the green wood
           It was the holly, holly, holly,
           And the first tree in the green wood
           It was the holly!

Solo: Now the holly bears a berry as black as the coal
           And Mary bore Jesus who died for us all.
Chorus: And Mary bore Jesus our Saviour for to be,
           And the first tree . . . *etc.*

Solo: Now the holly bears a berry as blood it is red;
           Then trust we our Saviour who rose from the de
Chorus: And Mary bore Jesus our Saviour for to be.
           And the first tree . . . *etc.*

In this carol, as in 'The Holly and The Ivy', the lines about ivy have been replaced by Church teaching. Holly is left alone. The reasons for that partial substitution are, first, its ease. Ivy is a symbol of woman, and therefore there is a facile transposition between her and Mary. Second, the taking-over of ivy's concluding part of each verse means that Church doctrine will control the whole song. The carol begins in the old way, which the peasants always sang, but then changes to the new doctrine, taking more and more of each generation with it.

But the miscegenation is now against all natural and artistic law. Holly is being matched with Mary, a symbolic male tree with a realistic mother. Her bearing of an unchanging, realistic son will not match holly's bearing of changing, symbolic berries.

None of the verses works as a whole. The two parts are not related. They are, indeed, so far apart that the most pathetic attempt is made to bridge them at the end:

Now the holly bears a berry as blood it is red;
Then trust we our Saviour who rose from the dead.

'Then' is trying to hold two opposed worlds together, the world of proud male sexuality and the world of Christian spirituosity. It's a lot to ask of a little word.

In none of the couplets at the beginning of each verse do the tenses match. Second lines should begin 'And Mary bears . . . '. Also, the bearing of Mary should fit the bearing of holly. Instead, the bearing of Jesus begins with 'wrapped up in silk', then goes to three descriptions from the crucifixion story—'died on the cross', 'died for us all' and 'rose from the dead'. These last three descriptive phrases do not fit holly's berry changing from green to black to red.

The first descriptive phrase doesn't fit fact either! Jesus was not wrapped up in silk! So why does the carol say he was, for surely everyone knows, (and knew), he was not? Because of the rhyme. The restorer was content with easy repetition of death and divinity in verses 2, 3 and 4, and the even more easy retention of the rhyme word in verse 1. He was lazy.

Let us leave out the Christian additions and consider the meaning of what is left. It is all about holly, showing a similar kind of development in him, as in 'The Holly and the Ivy'. Man's phallic development is said to be going from white to green to black to red.

Is that right? White and red we can accept, but green and black? We need confirmation that we have indeed found the theme of the original song. It is found in the chorus:

And the first tree that's in the green wood
It was the holly.

'First tree' doesn't mean anything literal, like being the first tree to bear berries. It is a parallel to 'The holly bears the crown.' It means holly is the Number One tree, the prime tree. So we do have the right theme, and this berry that changes is meant to be man's triumphant, potent symbol.

'Black' is an error. It fits neither berry nor man. 'Green' does fit berry and can fit man by being understood conventionally as 'young', rather than as true statement. It is possibly correct. In place of 'black' we must look at the holly berry and see that it becomes brownish as it changes from green to red. We have to refind the colour that fits berry and man, because the original word has been lost, forgotten, as the original meaning of the song was lost and forgotten. Occasionally, the pagan parts of the carols have been wrongly remembered, after the meaning of the whole song had been changed.

Holly's developing powers—white, green, brown, red—can only be matched by woman's, by ivy's. Each second line should begin 'And ivy bears . . .'. For the first verse, we are even given the key word 'silk' at the end of her line. For that verse, and all the others, we are also told that whatever she does bear is for 'our comfort'. So Ivy bears some attribute, of tree and woman, which matches man's and is for men's comfort, men's pleasure. The song must have been sung by a man, with the other men of the group as chorus.

The Holly Bears A Berry (Restored)

Solo Man:
Now the holly he bears a berry as white as the milk;
And ivy she bears a smooth leaf as soft as the silk.
Chorus Men:
And ivy she bears a smooth leaf our comfort for to be;
And the first tree that's in the green wood
It was the holly, holly, holly,
And the first tree that's in the green wood
It was the holly.

Solo Man:
Now the holly he bears a berry as green as the grass;
And ivy she bears a slim vine as she grows to a lass.
Chorus Men:
And ivy she bears a slim vine our comfort for to be;
And the first tree that's in the green wood
It was the holly, holly, holly,
And the first tree that's in the green wood
It was the holly.

Solo Man:
Now the holly he bears a berry as brown as the nut;
And ivy she bears a blossom at her breast it is put.
Chorus Men:
And ivy she bears a blossom our comfort for to be;
And the first tree that's in the green wood
It was the holly, holly, holly,
And the first tree that's in the green wood
It was the holly.

Solo Men:
Now the holly he bears a berry as red as the blood;
And ivy she bears a broad bush as high as he stood.
Chorus Men:
And ivy she bears a broad bush our comfort for to be;
And the first tree that's in the green wood
It was the holly, holly, holly,
And the first tree that's in the green wood
It was the holly.

The Seven Virgins

(Current Version)

All under the leaves, the leaves of life,
I met with virgins seven,
And one of them was Mary mild,
Our Lord's mother from heaven.

'O what are you seeking, you seven fair maids,
All under the leaves of life?
Come tell, come tell me what seek you
All under the leaves of life.'

'We're seeking for no leaves, Thomas,
But for a friend of thine;
We're seeking for sweet Jesus Christ
To be our guide and thine.'

'Go you down, go you down to yonder town,
And sit in the gallery;
And there you'll find sweet Jesus Christ
Nailed to a big yew-tree.'

So down they went to yonder town
As fast as foot could fall,
And many a grievous bitter tear
From the virgins' eyes did fall.

'O peace, mother, O peace, mother,
Your weeping doth me grieve;
O I must suffer this' he said
'For Adam and for Eve.'

'O how can I my weeping leave,
Or my sorrows undergo,
Whilst I do see my own Son die,
When sons I have no mo'?'

'Dear mother, dear mother, you must take John,
All for to be your son,
And he will comfort you sometimes,
Mother, as I have done.'

'O come, thou John Evangelist,
Thou'rt welcome unto me,
But more welcome my own dear son,
That I nursed upon my knee.'

Then he laid his head on his right shoulder
Seeing death it struck him nigh;
'The Holy Ghost be with your soul—
I die, mother dear, I die.'

O the rose, the rose, the gentle rose,
And the fennel that grows so green!
God give us grace in every place
To pray for our king and queen.

Furthermore for our enemies all
Our prayers they should be strong.
Amend, Good Lord! your charity
Is the ending of my song.

(Last verse but one as sung by the Watersons in their record *Frost and Fire*)

The end of the narrative is from the Bible (St John's Gospel) but the beginning and the middle are not. There is no Bible story of Mary and six other virgins seeking Christ under the leaves of life. Mary and the other women knew perfectly well where Christ was. Thomas did not have to inform them. They were present at a distance when he was crucified. They did not sit in a gallery. Christ was not nailed to a big yew-tree. So, where did this beginning and middle come from?

My thesis is that they come from a folk-song. As in the two previous carols of holly and ivy, I think a Christian propagandist has rewritten a pagan song. He has retained the beginning and some of the middle. But at the end he has inserted a Gospel story and a Christian moral.

The result of his substitutions is to break the narrative. It no longer is a story. The song begins with seven virgins. What happened to them? The questioner of them is identified as Thomas. What happened to him? How will the virgins find Jesus if they sit in the gallery? What is the relevance of the ending.

'O the rose, the rose, and the gentle rose,
And the fennel that grows so green'?

Why are seven virgins seeking for Jesus Christ under the leaves of life? That, surely, cannot be realism. There must be symbolism involved there.

The leaves of life grow on the Tree of Life. The current version, by repeating 'leaves', has obscured, deliberately or accidentally, the symbol. The Tree of Life is an image of generation in many countries. The pagan Vikings, who brought us wassailing, called it Ygdrasil. So this tree is linking us with our early culture, with Woden's Day and Thor's Day. These leaves show how old the song is.

It seems to me a denial of life, and of logic, to answer that virgins are seeking there, in that most fecund place, Jesus Christ to be their guide. That must be Christian rewriting. What grows under the leaves of any tree? Its fruit, its berries. And the fruit, the berries, that virgins are seeking under the leaves of the Tree of Life can only be—babies.

Why are there *seven* virgins? The significance of the number seven is derived from the fact that there are seven openings in the human body. This human significance can become magical by linking it to the prevention of disease. It can become vague, as its physical origin is forgotten, and come to mean something mystically human. Here the seven virgins are typical of all virgins, mystically human, virgins present and to come. So the story of only one of them is told.

Now there is a clear beginning of their story from which much can be deduced. But there is a clear ending to their story as well. This carol is like a tangle of string, but the two ends can be seen. By following first one, then the other, the tangled web can be unravelled.

That other end is

'O the rose, the rose, the gentle rose
And the fennel that grows so green'

('strong' in another version). That shows the story was a love story. The rose is a symbol of love. This is the gentle rose. It is, therefore, a symbol of woman's love, while the fennel, either so green or so strong, is man's love, for 'green' can mean, by convention, 'youthful'. Fennel symbolized masculine strength. Longfellow says gladiators ate it

. . . with their daily food,
And he who battled and subdued
A wreath of fennel wore.

It was sacred to Sabazios, an Eastern god like Dionysos, whose emblem was a serpent and who was always represented with horns. Sabbazia were nocturnal orgies. Fennel must have come to mean that kind of virile strength in the West as in the East. Ophelia gave it to Hamlet.

So here is a song that begins with virgins' search for children and ends with the symbols of the sexes. Who are the virgins, or the one particularized, going to find to love? The character called Thomas. He was lost in the Christian rewriting. His place, his words, were re-allocated to Jesus. He must be reinstated—under another name, of course.

Where will he advise this weeping virgin to go and look for children? His original advice must have indicated a tree, for the Christian rewriter followed that with his 'big, yew tree'. Now, though the yew-tree was originally planted in graveyards as a sign of fertile life, because of all its red berries, it is not the tree particularly wanted here. The man (Thomas) will say that children can be found only on the tree that is specifically male. That tree is the same holly we sang about in the previous two carols.

The virgin runs to the holly, weeping. The story has to end as a love story. So that weeping affects the man deeply, and he says 'O peace, O peace, you weeping maid [not 'mother'] Your sorrow doth me grieve.' And how will he go on? There is only one person who can comfort her, and it isn't John. It must be to him that she says: 'Thou'rt welcome unto me.' Then it will be her own dear son, whom she has been seeking from the beginning, who will be even more welcome when she nurses him on her knee. She lays her head on her

167

lover's shoulder, and now woman's gentle love, plus man's virile strength, can end the song.

Given the meaning, the form will follow. The Christian spoiled the form. Rhymes are simply the same word, repeated, in verses 2 and 5. Lines are far too long to scan—the need to put 'mother' for 'maid' has led to the extra syllables in 'Dear mother, dear mother, you must take John.' And the last six lines don't follow the meaning at all. They are the addition of a monarchist beggar with pacifist sympathies! But the form can be remade by anyone who cherishes the original song and wants it sung again.

The Tree of Life
(Restored)

All under the leaves of the Tree of Life,
I met with virgins seven,
And one of them was weeping wild,
And her hair was unkempen.

'O what are you seeking, you pretty maiden,
All under the leaves so green?'
'I am seeking for no leaves, Robin,
But for my babes unseen.'

'Go up, go up, to yon hill-top,
And search for the fairest tree,
And there you'll find your children dear
Set on the red holly.'

So up she went to yon hill-top
As fast as she could run,
And many a bitter and a grievous tear
From that virgin's eyes did come.

'O peace, O peace, you weeping maid,
Your sorrow doth me grieve;
You shall not suffer this' I said,
'If I may give relief.'

'O how can I my weeping leave,
Or my sorrow overcome,
When I do see my time pass by,
And I am all alone?'

'Dear maid, dear maid, you shall take me
To be your own husband,
And I will comfort you sometimes
When you are all alone.'

'O come, Robin', and me she kissed,
'You're welcome unto me;
As welcome as my own dear son
When I nurse him on my knee.'

She laid her head on my right shoulder,
Seeing love had struck her nigh;
Now peace and rest come in your breast,
As darling down you lie!

O the rose, the gentle rose,
The prickle strong as the thorn!
O may maids find true hearts to love
So their children can be born!

THE TREE OF LIFE

All und-er the leaves of the Tree of Life I met with vir- gins seven And one of them was weep- ing wild And her hair was un- Kemp- ed

Yule Carols and
Wassails

Joys Seven

(Current version)

The first good joy that Mary had
It was the joy of one;
To see the blessed Jesus Christ
When he was first her son:

Chorus:
When he was first her son, good man,
And blessed may he be,
Both Father, Son, and Holy Ghost,
To all eternity.

The next good joy that Mary had
It was the joy of two;
To see her own son Jesus Christ
To make the lame to go.

Chorus:
To make the lame to go, good man,
And blessed may he be,
Both Father, Son, and Holy Ghost,
To all eternity.

The next good joy that Mary had
It was the joy of three;
To see her own son Jesus Christ
To make the blind to see.

Chorus:
To make the blind to see, good man,
And blessed may he be,
Both Father, Son, and Holy Ghost,
To all eternity.

172

The next good joy that Mary had
It was the joy of four;
To see the blessed Jesus Christ
To read the Bible o'er.

Chorus:
To read the Bible o'er, good man, etc.

Verses five, six, and seven follow the pattern. They
are—

5. To bring the dead alive.
6. Upon the crucifix.
7. To wear the crown of heaven.

OTHER VERSIONS:

'The dinner that the little bird's (the wren's) carcass
will provide is such that the Manx would invite King
and Queen, and yet have enough over to give 'eyes to
the blind, legs to the lame, and pluck to the poor'.*

I think everyone will agree that the sixth joy of Mary—

To see her own son Jesus Christ
Upon the crucifix

is very odd. Is it that taste in 'religious joy' has
changed? Or that someone couldn't find another
Christian rhyme-word to 'six'?

Joy four is not only odd: it's wrong! Of course Jesus
didn't 'read the Bible o'er'. The Bible was compiled
centuries after the death of Christ. Is it that the
peasants didn't know their history? The effect of the
line is to stress the importance of Bible-reading. Who
gains by that?

*(Oxford Dictionary of Nursery Rhymes)

As always, my hypothesis, that the traditional carols have been altered by Christian propagandists, must contest the alternative hypothesis that pious but ignorant (and stupid) peasants made them. So, if I can show that doctrine—the Church view—is being propounded, that is a sign that Churchmen did the alteration. They gain. Peasants don't.

The other joys pass a first examination, but the chorus doesn't. In that, Jesus is blessed twice, first as 'he', then as 'the Son'—

When he was first her son, good man,
And blessed may he be,
Both Father, Son, and Holy Ghost,
To all eternity.

Secondly, 'both' is made to apply to three personages! Such grammatical errors often reveal alteration, as in the famous 'Holly and Ivy' first verse. Again, these chorus lines are straight doctrine lines. But what is the 'good man' doing amongst them? Is it a meaningless tag? Or one peasant telling his boorish neighbour? Or is it a remnant of the original song, which no longer fits because of the alteration of the other chorus lines?

Another grammatical point arises in that first verse—as it does in verse 6 (the 'crucifix' one). It is, that the pattern of the last lines is to begin with a verb in the infinitive— 'To make the lame to go', 'To make the blind to see', 'To wear the crown of heaven'. But in verses 1 and 6 that pattern is not followed. That is another sign of alteration in both those verses.

Those are small points, straws in the wind. But our first mechanical examination of the seven joys—to see if they were Biblical, historical and self-consistent—passed over a deeper objection to all of them. These joys of Mary are, in fact, not her own joys at all. They are the powers of Jesus. That change of meaning is covered up by the 'to see'—that she saw him use those powers. But that still doesn't make them her own joys. Mary's own joys are to conceive a son, to bear him, to give him the breast, to look after him, to teach him, to follow him. Her first joy, scripturally speaking, is to learn that she has been chosen, not 'to see' anything. Her joy at his birth would be more than to see him 'when he was first her son'. All her supposed joys are too detached from her.

That thinking brings our mechanical examination to life. Was Mary recorded as present at all Christ's miracles? If not, how is it known that she saw them?

Is Mary not being substituted for any woman? She took the place of ivy in the holly and ivy carols, of the leader of 'The Seven Virgins', of the heroine of 'I Sing Of A Maiden'. Was the song's subject not the seven joys of a woman? Their replacement with doctrine would account for some of the smaller discrepancies. The censorship of the maternal and sexual joys of woman would also account for the deeper inconsistencies. The song's original subject would account for the song's former popularity. It was one of the most popular carols, according to the editor of the OBC. It isn't now. A badly-made traditional carol is a popular folk-song indoctrinated. Then it becomes less popular, until it is not sung at all.

Thinking of any woman's maternal and sexual joys, I remembered the powers of Jenny Wren, the pagan bird-symbol of woman. She, too, could make the lame go, the blind see and—not 'read the Bible o'er' but—'give pluck to the poor'. She could bring the dead alive. She could make a better rhyme with 'six' than 'crucifix'. She could see someone in the heaven of her love. Those are the real joys of woman. So I restored the powers, the joys and the praise to her name.

The Seven Joys of Jenny (Restored)

The first good joy that Jenny had
It was the joy of one,
To see the power her nesty had
To make to speak the dumb.

Chorus:
To make to speak the dumb, b . . . boom,
And blessed may she be,
Both birdy, nest,—and loving song—
For ever night and day.

The next good joy that Jenny had
It was the joy of two,
To see the power her nesty had
To make the lame to go.

Chorus:
To make the lame to go, b . . . boom,
And blessed may she be,
Both birdy, nest—and loving song—
For ever night and day.

The next good joy that Jenny had
It was the joy of three,
To see the power her nesty had
To make the blind to see.

Chorus:
To make the blind to see, b . . . boom *etc.*

The next good joy that Jenny had
It was the joy of four,
To see the power her nesty had
To give pluck to the poor.

176

Chorus:
To give pluck to the poor, b . . . boom *etc.*

The next good joy that Jenny had
It was the joy of five,
To see the power her nesty had
To bring the dead alive.

Chorus:
To bring the dead alive, b . . . boom *etc.*

The next good joy that Jenny had
It was the joy of six,
To see the power her nesty had
To stand up stumps like sticks.

Chorus:
To stand up stumps like sticks, b . . . boom *etc.*

The next good joy that Jenny had
It was the joy of seven,
To see the power her nesty had
To raise man into heaven.

Chorus:
To raise man into heaven, b . . . boom,
And blessed may she be,
Both birdy, nest,—and loving song—
For ever night and day.

God Rest You Merry, Gentlemen
(Current Version)

God rest you merry, gentlemen,
Let nothing you dismay,
Remember Christ our Saviour
Was born on Christmas Day,
To save poor souls from Satan's power
Which had long time gone astray,

And it's tidings of comfort and joy,
      comfort and joy,
And it's tidings of comfort and joy.

From God that is our Father,
The blessed angels came,
Unto some certain shepherds
With tidings of the same;
That there was born in Bethlehem
The son of God by name.

And it's tidings of comfort and joy *etc.*

Go, fear not, said God's angels,
Let nothing you affright,
For there is born in Bethlehem,
Of a pure virgin bright,
One able to advance you
And throw down Satan quite.

And it's tidings of comfort and joy *etc.*

The shepherds at those tidings
Rejoiced much in mind,
And left their flocks a-feeding
In tempest storms of wind,
And strait they came to Bethlehem,
The Son of God to find.

And it's tidings of comfort and joy *etc.*

Now when they came to Bethlehem,
Where our sweet Saviour lay,
They found him in a manger
Where oxen feed on hay,
The blessed Virgin kneeling down
Unto the Lord did pray.

And it's tidings of comfort and joy *etc.*

With sudden joy and gladness
The shepherds were beguiled,
To see the Babe of Israel,
Before his mother mild,
On them with joy and cheerfulness
Rejoice each mother's child.

And it's tidings of comfort and joy *etc.*

Now to the Lord sing praises,
All you within this place,
Like we true loving brethren,
Each other to embrace,
For the merry time of Christmas
Is drawing on apace.

And it's tidings of comfort and joy *etc.*

God bless the ruler of this house,
And send him long to reign,
And many a merry Christmas
May live to see again.
Among your friends and kindred,
That live both far and near,
And God send you a happy New Year.

OTHER VERSIONS:

The carol has two versions in the *OBC*. I have quoted No. 12. The other, No. 11, differs as follows: it has an additional verse (its verse 2, of which I made nothing); its verse 4 (verse 3 of No. 12) has:

This day is born a Saviour
Of virtue, power, and might

(of which I took the rhyme-word 'might');
it has no parallel to verses 6 and 8.

The ending of this carol is similar to that of two wassails. The Wassail Song (No. 15, *OBC*) has:

God bless the master of this house,
The mistress also,
And all the little children
That round the table go.

Chorus:
Love and joy come to you,
And to you your Wassail too,
And God bless you and send you
A happy New Year.

And all your kin and kinsfolk,
That dwell both far and near;
I wish you a merry Christmas
And a happy New Year.

The 'Sussex Mummers' Carol' has (vv. 4–6):

God bless the mistress of this house
With gold chain round her breast;
Where'er her body sleeps or wakes,
Lord, send her soul to rest.

God bless the master of this house
With happiness beside;
Where'er his body rides or walks
Lord Jesus be his guide.

God bless your house, your children too,
Your cattle and your store;
The Lord increase you day by day,
And send you more and more.

I hope I have shown by the quotation from the two wassails, that this carol, too, must have been a wassail. If a Christian carol has a wassail ending, either it must have been a wassail, or an inappropriate wassail ending must have somehow got attached to it. But the wassail ending is found in both versions, though reduced to only one verse in one of them. That, to me, proves that it was the real ending which could not be detached. Also, one of the tunes shows it was a wassail. 'It is a favourite with English folk-singers, and is often used in Wassail songs,' Cecil Sharp wrote.

So the gentlemen are not in church but in a hall,

surrounded by 'true loving brethren', and the whole company is being wassailed. First, the singers wish that they may stay merry. So they are merry already!

For tonight we'll merry, merry be
For tonight we'll merry, merry be
For tonight we'll merry, merry be
And tomorrow we'll be sober.

That is the right tone of a wassail. Drinking from the wassail bowl was always part of the celebration. To wish someone merry is no Christian wish. A Christian would wish them to be good. But after the striking first two lines, which people still love, there seems nothing left of the original wassail until the last two verses. There is the difficulty!

But let us be unconquered like the sun, brave like the holly, and merry like the gentlemen. We have a great external clue to the subject of the song. The tidings of comfort and joy—which conclude every verse—must have been that the sun is coming back. That would be the theme celebrated when wassails were sung. What did the Christian rewriter make of it? He put something about Bethlehem each time! His repetition is due to the repetition of the wassail. Every rewriter is influenced by the original writing.

Knowing the subject, we may also seek the pattern of wassails from others of them. The best known I have quoted in the 'Other Versions'. They well-wish the principal individuals of the household, then relatives, and then farm animals, and crops. The Gloucestershire Wassail well-wishes the animals first before going to the master and mistress.

All progress round the audience so that everyone gets the good wish. It's obviously vital that no one should be left out. Here the singers begin with the gentlemen, so must proceed to the next group, the ladies; after them, the young men, the girls, the children, the kinsfolk. That will fit on to verse 7, where all are invited to embrace.

We must search for signs that this is indeed the pattern. Unfortunately, verse 2 does not follow it. It is a repetition, only, of the good news, I restore it in the notes to the wassail. But verse 3 has 'Let nothing you affright.' That does parallel 'Let nothing you dismay.' It keeps the pattern. The next group is liable to be affrighted. That group must be the ladies. Therefore the wassail is indeed progressing from the gentlemen, who are not to be dismayed, to the ladies, who aren't to be frightened.

Verses 4, 5 and 6 do not have any well-wishing line and do not seem addressed to groups. The re-writing has been more thorough. But why is it so bad? Why did the friar write 'Rejoiced much *in mind*'? Where else could anyone have rejoiced? Why write 'In tempest storms of *wind*'? Because of the rhymes, of course. He wanted to keep the rhyme-words and was ready to renounce reason—never his friend—to do so. 'The shepherds were beguiled.' Were they? 'Rejoice each mother's child.' They only? 'Throw down Satan quite.' That's so bad it's the friar's own! The other version is even worse: 'The friends of Satan quite'. Does anyone pretend the folk wrote that? Or anyone who was writing his own composition? It must be a hasty addition.

But I re-took the other rhyme-words. All I had to do with them was—a better job than the monk! For I had the conclusive conclusion, and the two-line beginning, and the pattern of the verses. Any careful restoration of the original wassail must be better than a careless conversion into a Christmas carol.

Now Make You Merry, Gentlemen! (Restored)

Now make you merry, gentlemen,
Let winter not dismay,
For the sure Sun does now return
Upon this very day,
To keep us all from dark and cold
He has not gone away,
O, tidings of comfort and joy,
        comfort and joy,
O, tidings of comfort and joy!

[*See note about verse 2*]

Now make you merry, ladies,
Let darkness not affright,
For the sure Sun does now return
So strong and bold and bright,
To keep us all from dark and cold
He has his manly might,
O, tidings of comfort and joy,
        comfort and joy,
O, tidings of comfort and joy!

Now make you merry, bachelors,
Let need not numb your mind,
For the sure Sun does now return
In fire and flesh and wine,
To keep us all from dark and cold
He has a way to find,
O, tidings of comfort and joy,
        comfort and joy,
O, tidings of comfort and joy!

Now make you merry, maidens,
Let damp not spoil your lay,
For the sure Sun does now return
You'll dance upon the hay,
To keep us all from dark and cold
He'll give you what you pray,
O, tidings of comfort and joy,
             comfort and joy,
O, tidings of comfort and joy!

Now make you merry, children,
Let fear not you beguile,
For the sure Sun does now return
You'll eat and play and smile,
To keep us all from dark and cold
There's presents for each child,
O, tidings of comfort and joy,
             comfort and joy,
O, tidings of comfort and joy!

Now to the Sun sing praises
All you within this place,
And like a loving company
Each other do embrace,
The heart-felt time of the New Year
Is drawing on apace,
O, tidings of comfort and joy,
             comfort and joy,
O, tidings of comfort and joy!

[*See note about verse 8*]

Note: I have omitted verses 2 and 8 because they are superfluous. They belong to other wassails. They are:

Verse 2.
To heaven where he's Unconquered,
The rising sun then came,
And he has shown to everyone
Good news ever the same,
That each New Year he does return
According to his name,
O, tidings *etc.*

Verse 8.
God bless the ruler of this house
And send him long to reign,
And many a merry Yule-time
He'll live to see again,
Amongst his friends and kindred
He ever shall remain,
O, tidings *etc.*

Also, I have preferred 'In fire and flesh and wine' (verse 4) to some line like 'To warm this shrivelling wind', which would have retained the given rhyme-word.

Welcome Yule

(Current Version)

Solo:
Welcome Yule, thou merry man,
In worship of this holy day!
Welcome Yule, welcome Yule.

Welcome be thou, heaven-king,
Welcome born in one morning,
Welcome for whom we shall sing
Chorus:
Welcome Yule, welcome Yule.

Welcome be ye, Stephen and John,
Welcome Innocents everyone,
Welcome Thomas, martyr one:
Chorus:
Welcome Yule, welcome Yule.

Welcome be ye, good New Year,
Welcome Twelfth Day, both *in fere.* (together)
Welcome saintes *lief* and dear: (beloved)
Chorus:
Welcome Yule, welcome Yule.

Welcome be ye, Candlemas,
Welcome be ye, queen of bliss,
Welcome both to more and less:
Chorus:
Welcome Yule, welcome Yule.

Welcome be ye, that are here,
Welcome all, and make good cheer,
Welcome all another year!
Chorus:
Welcome Yule, welcome Yule, welcome Yule.

OTHER VERSIONS:

Chorus:
Welcome Yule, in glad array,
In worship of the holiday.
Welcome Yule, for ever and aye.

Welcome be thou, good New Year,
Welcome the Twelve Days, ever,
Welcome be ye, all that be here,
Welcome Yule for ever and aye.*

'Welcome Yule, thou merry man'. Then saints and martyrs out! You come too late. Yule was pre-Christian.

Maybe his name survived? Maybe his song did, too! Till some priest got hold of it, in the thirteenth century, and changed some of it.

Verse 1 is still his. Yule was born that morning. Jesus wasn't. Yule's holy day was the day of his birth, of the sun's return. December 25 was declared the birthday of the Unconquered Sun, way back before the Christian conversion. It's the sun who is so welcome, in real life; and in this carol. And Yule is the sun's personification—the sun often has a man's face. So, in comes the original Father Christmas figure.

But verse 2 has been changed. It's obvious who changed it, and why. A welcomer of saints, martyrs, and innocents. Yule never came with them. He was merry. The priest preferred to meet his own kind.

So, welcome Thomas, if you're the doubter, in verse

*(No. 7 *The Early English Carols*)

188

3. I always liked your common sense. But you and your friends have all come to the wrong party. The queen of bliss also. I doubt if 'bliss' is more than a quick disguise to get her in. It's not Mary's usual description. The mother of sorrows?

But without any doubt, welcome good New Year. That's a touch of the original again. How nice to have it called 'good'. That's back to the old values. The pagan Scots, still keep it up. For days, too. It was a twelve-day feast in pagan times.

Candlemas? He's another gate-crasher. Candlemas is February 2nd! If the others have come to the wrong place, Candlemas has come on the wrong day! Priests tried to extend the 'holy season' to Candlemas, because then the Virgin Mary became the central figure. But no festival—not even a pagan one—lasted forty days.

Then, finally, the right people again, everyone that's here, ordinary people, us! And we are to make good cheer another year. As we always do.

So, the current version is the mixture as before. All we have to do is keep the merry man, and suggest to the saints and martyrs they'd be happier in a hymn.

What do we put in their place? First, what is Yule, even now, after hundreds of years, still known for? The Yule Log. That must have been in. And where was it? It was in that verse about Candlemas. Candles, flames, Yule Log—that's how his mind worked. That's why he put Candlemas in, though it's so obviously wrong.

And all the other Christian late-comers, who or what did they replace? The chorus tells us. 'Welcome Yule, welcome Yule' can only follow verses about Yule. We've just found one about his log. Others will be about his 'glad array', his return 'for ever and aye'. He, the founder of the feast, its personification, has come to the people in the hall. Their carol is for him alone; for him with them.

Welcome Yule
(Restored)

Welcome Yule, old heaven's king,
Welcome Yule, born this morning,
Welcome Yule, man full-smiling,
Welcome, welcome Yule.

Chorus:
Welcome Yule, thou merry man,
Welcome Yule, spend here thy span.

Welcome Yule, red-robéd one,
Welcome Yule, come from the sun,
Welcome Yule, our hearts' crimson,
Welcome, welcome Yule.
Chorus:

Welcome Yule, good-news bearer,
Welcome Yule, of the New Year,
Welcome Yule, twelve days you'll hear
Welcome, welcome Yule.
Chorus:

Welcome Yule, thy log's aflame,
Welcome Yule, thy fire doth gain,
Welcome Yule, warmth grows again,
Welcome, welcome Yule.
Chorus:

Welcome Yule, enter this hall,
Welcome Yule, centre of all,
Welcome Yule, our first Carol,
Welcome, welcome Yule.
Chorus:

Welcome Yule, as ever was,
Welcome Yule, as ever thus,
Welcome Yule, as ever must,
Welcome, welcome Yule.
Chorus:

Welcome Yule, come well in here,
Welcome Yule, make us good cheer,
Welcome Yule, once more thou'rt here,
Welcome, welcome Yule.

WELCOME YULE

Music © 1985 Gloria Newton

The Early English Carols
No. 457 (Modernized English)

Chorus:
'Kyrie, so kyrie' [Lord]
Jankin sings merrily
with *'Eleison'*. [have mercy]

As I went on Yule Day in our procession
Knew I jolly Jankin by his merry tone.
'Kyrie Eleison.'

Jankin began the office on the Yule Day,
'And yet methinks it does me good' so merry 'gan he
    to say
'Kyrie Eleison'.

Jankin read the Epistle full fair and full well,
'And yet methinks it does me good as ever I have *sel'*
                             [good luck]
'Kyrie Eleison.'

Jankin at the Sanctus cracked a merry note,
'And yet methinks it does me good; I paid for his *cote'*
                                [coat?]
'Kyrie Eleison.'

Jankin cracked notes, a *hundred on a knot,* *
And yet he chopped them smaller than herbs for the pot.
'Kyrie Eleison.'

Jankin at the Agnus bore the *pax-brede*   [silver disc]
He twinkled, but said nought, and on my foot he tread.
'Kyrie Eleison.'

* The short notes of polyphonic music

Benedicamus Domino; Christ from shame me shield,
Deo Gracias, as well; alas, I go with child.
'Kyrie Eleison.'

OTHER VERSIONS:

'What is being farced is definitely the Kyrie of the Mass . . . In the burden (Chorus), there is probably a pun on the girl's name Alison'—Greene. *'Alison'* is first spelt 'aleyson' in the manuscript.

If it weren't for that last verse, I'd be told I had a dirty mind. 'The Carol shows the earthy, natural joy people felt in their Christianity in medieval times. How happily they sang and smiled at Mass! Many courtships did begin then, you know, and Mother Church does not condemn them.' No one can say anything as soft as that after the last verse.

Jankin and Alison made love on Christmas Day in the church. Is that sacrilegious? It depends on the religion.

Christmas Day was Yule Day. On that day English people worshipped The Great Mother. 'The very night we so deeply revere they called Mother's Night'— Bede, quoted in *How They Lived* (Blackwell). You can't have a Great Mother without a Great Lover. Jankin, on Yule Day, in the Church these carols belong to, was religious. There used to be what are now called 'religious prostitutes' in Greece and Rome. They were really disciples.

If it weren't for Jankin and Alison, and generations of couples like them, marriages wouldn't take place in church today. The whole ceremony is a pagan survival. There's no hint of how to conduct one in the New Testament. They don't take place at all in Christian heaven, you may remember. Birth, marriage death, 'and thoughts of these', are contained in church now because they were expressed there then.

194

The cock was on the steeple, the ancestors were under the floor.

Alison, at the end, is confused by the two differing religions. The old one, *'Deo gracias'*, 'Thank God I'm pregnant.' The new one, 'Women is a temple built over a sewer' (St. Jerome), 'Alas, I go with child.' The old one is now becoming modern, because it's natural. The new one is now becoming old-fashioned.

The conflict between the two led to the farcing. Virginity, as virtue, is farcical. It's like making yourself a eunuch for the kingdom of heaven's sake.

Someone saw that *Eleison* was like Alison, 'pistle like pestle, pax-brede like peace-bread, office like office. He responded with his own understanding of 'It does me good.' He made a double-meaning Mass— until his meaning was delivered and borne out.

But some of his double-meanings have been lost. Where is it in the chorus? If it's only in *'Eleison'* being like Alison that's not good enough to be sung verse after verse. *'Kyrie'* must have a similar-sounding word, too. As many as possible—that's the merry motive of all double meanings.

Then the verses have to be put back in their right order. Jankin wouldn't twinkle, say nothing and tread on her foot at the end of the service. He'd do it when the organ was playing, at the beginning.

And he needs a good tune. Happily, I found 'The Ball Of Kirremuir' rising up in me, to meet his words sinking in. Their fusion meant changes. It always does. Ask Alison.

Jolly Jankin's Carol
(Restored: Tune: 'The Ball of Kirremuir')

Solo: As I went up on Yule Day in the Church
procession,
I knew young jolly Jankin by his eyes'
confession,

Chorus: Singing 'Higheree, so higheree,
And higheree again',
Jankin sings it merrily
With Alison.

Solo: Beginning of the service he upraised the
silver rod,
He winked at me, but he said nought, and on
my foot he trod,
Chorus: Singing 'Higheree *etc.*

Solo: He began the Office with me on that
very first of days,
'I always think it does me good to stretch
myself' he says,
Chorus: Singing 'Higheree *etc*

Solo: Jankin read the Lesson very long and
very well,
'I always think it does me good to start in
the middle,'
Chorus: Singing 'Higheree *etc.*

Solo: Jankin played me all his staff notes.
'twas a hundred for each hymn.
I always think it does me good to quicken
the rhythm.
Chorus: Singing 'Higheree *etc.*

Solo: At the end of our sweet Sanctus song, he
      hit the topmost note,
      'I always think it does me good to sing
      with all my throat.'
Chorus: Singing 'Higheree *etc.*

Solo: At the end of our communion he did
      give me the peace-bread,
      He gasped, he sighed, he kissed me, then he
      left me on the bed.
Chorus: Singing 'Higheree *etc.*

Solo: God bless me now, and Jesus too, I hope
      from shame they'll shield.
      Thanks be to God for Jankin, and his
      jolly, spankin' child!
Chorus: Singing 'Higheree, so higheree,
      And higheree again'
      Jankin sings it merrily With Alison.

JOLLY JANKIN'S CAROL

King Herod and the Cock
(Current Version)

There was a star in David's land,
So bright it did appear
Into King Herod's chamber,
And brightly it shined there.

The wise men soon espied it,
And told the king on high,
A princely babe was born that night
No king could e'er destroy.

'If this be true' King Herod said,
'As thou hast told to me,
This roasted cock that lies in the dish
Shall crow full *fences* three.'   [times]

The cock soon *thrustened* and feathered well.
                                               [thrust out]
By the work of God's own hand,
And he did crow full fences three,
In the dish where he did stand.

OTHER VERSIONS:

To admiration rose
The naked cock, his youthful plumes
Around his body shows.

                        (*c.*1800)

There is no such story in the Bible. So where did it
come from? From the Danes. 'The cock story has been
traced to *c.*1200 in Prior's *Ancient Danish Ballads,*' says
the footnote in the *OBC*. The ballad will be older than
its first trace. Before 1200 the Danish folk were pagan.

198

King Cnut's men must have brought it to England. They landed from their longships, horn helmets on their heads, roaring out the song of the cock. Then, after some hundreds of years, someone converted it to a Christian carol.

Now we know its history, we can restore it. The cold water-sprinkler obviously put 'David's land' instead of 'Danish land'; 'King Herod' instead of the 'King of the Danes'.

If we replace all his equivalents, the story is 'There was a bright star over Denmark, it shone into the king's chamber. Some wise old Danes saw it, and told him "A young prince is born, that not even you can kill." "If that's true," replied the king, "this roast cock in the dish shall crow three times." Then the cock thrust out, grew his feathers again, and crowed three times in the dish where he stood.' You can't keep a good cock down, even if you're the king!

How much clearer the story is when it's written as prose! Even the thrusting out of the cock had been made difficult to understand. Rhyme had been divorced from reason by Bible-story-telling.

The star—let's follows its guiding. It's the morning star (and the evening star), the star of love. Venus, we call it. The Danes called Venus Frigge. They meant the same frigging thing as we do. When it shines, the cock crows.

After the Danes had settled in England long enough for them to speak English, they sang that the star shines over every land. For her power was the same power. And the Angles and Saxons, from nearby Germany, also thought a cock shouldn't fall at the first fence. That's why they put him on the church steeple.

The King and the Cock (Restored)

There is a star over every land,
So bright it doth appear,
Into each bedroom window
At cock-crow it shines clear.

The married men first spied it,
And told to all their joy,
'A star-raised power comes up each dawn
No king can ever destroy.'

'If this be true' the king did say,
When he did hear their cry,
'This roasted cock that lies in the dish
Shall crow three times on high.'

The cock thrust out, and feathered well,
By the power over every land,
And he did crow three times on high
In the dish where he did stand.

The Boar's Head Carol
(Current Version)

The boar's head in hand bear I,
Bedecked with bays and rosemary;
And I pray you, my masters, be merry,
Quot estis in convivio. [so many as are in the feast]

Chorus:
Caput apri defero,   [The boar's head I bring]
Reddens laudes Domino   [Giving praises to God]

200

The boar's head, as I understand,
Is the rarest dish in all this land,
Which thus bedecked with a gay garland,
Let us *servire cantico*.   [Let us serve with a song]

Our Steward hath provided this
In honour of the King of bliss,
Which on this day to be served is,
In Reginensi atrio.   [In the Queen's hall]

OTHER VERSIONS:

For restored-verse 1:
'I pray you all with me to sing'.

Chorus:
Hey, hey, hey, hey,
The boar's head is arméd gay.

For verse 2:
The boar's head I understand
Is in great use in all this land,
Look, wherever it is found.

Or is the bravest dish in all this land.

For verse 3:
A boar is a sovereign beast
And acceptable in every feast,
So might this Lord be, to most and least.

For verse 4:
The boar's head that we bring here
Betokens a prince without peer.

For verse 5:
Lords, knights, and squires,
Parsons, priests, and vicars,
The boar's head is the first meal.

For verse 6:
The boar's head I dare well say
Soon after the Twelfth Day
He takes his leave and goes away.

For verse 7:
Be glad, lords, both more and less,
The boar's head with mustard.

Alternative chorus:
Po, po, po, po,
I love brawn and so do more.

'The boar's head was the favoured dish in the great Yule festival of the Northmen'—Chamber's *Dictionary*. Then this is a pagan carol.

It has to be restored because it has fallen into the hands of the Churchmen. The current version, in the OBC, is from Queen's College, Oxford, where all the fellows were clergy. It was they who substituted Latin for English. It was they who wrote that the boar's head was 'in honour of the King of bliss'. In honour of Jesus? King of bliss? The boar's head?

We can begin to restore the carol to our mother-tongue if we can understand why it was the favoured dish. It is not the best part of the boar, by Friar Tuck's standards. Pig's head, it is called today, and no one wants to buy it. It was eaten by the Vikings not for its savour but for its vigour. Eating the head or the heart of an animal was to incorporate its life-powers. What life-powers has a boar? Its tucks—'armed gay'. They are like the antlers of a stag.

The tusks signify two qualities—fighting strength and sexual strength. So the boar can be a crest on a shield, like a bull. Or it can be any man's manly crest, like every other horn. The line in the first verse of the current version shows the two meanings: 'Bedecked with bays and rosemary·' Bays are for the fighting hero, rosemary for the loving one. 'I pray you, love, remember,' says Ophelia to Hamlet, giving him rosemary. She meant remembrance of their love.

So the great head is garlanded, and the white tusks are gilded. This is, literally, a love-feast. 'The boar's head is the first meal,' says verse 5 of the 'Other Versions'. First meal means both best meal, and the meal that begins. So it's a piece of boar's cheek to tell that to parsons, priests and vicars. They are reminded of Adam and Eve.

A red love apple is always put in the boar's mouth. And that is why, in verse 7, 'Other Versions', mustard is put with him. Not primarily for its taste. Because 'He's mustard!' Hot stuff! Even the 'hey' of the 'Other Version' chorus is double meaning. Love's always been on the hay. Once there is a meaningful symbol, it grows, like a rose.

People begin to be merry, to take the tone, once they know what kind of a song they're singing.

'The boar's head, I understand
Is in great use in all this land.'

They'll sing that merrily enough. The clergy—fellows of Queens killed the joke, putting 'rarest* dish' in their version. But 'use' is right. Merry England. It goes with

'Soon after the Twelfth Day
He takes his leave and goes away.'

* Greene prints 'bravest'—handsomest. 'Rarest' is a lot less brave.

To be in use for twelve days, isn't bad. Men smile, become enthusiastic. 'I love brawn, and so do more.'

For all who love brawn, or crackling, here is my restoration of the Vikings' theme. They wore horns on their hats.

The Boar's Head Carol (Restored)

The boar's brave head on high I bring
With garlands gay, remembering
He makes us laugh and dance and sing,
Of merry-making, he is king.

Chorus:
With hay! and hay! and hay! and hay!
The boar's head is on high today.

The boar's head, as I understand,
Is greatly used in all this land,
Wherever he doth stay and stand
He is well-loved on every hand.

Chorus:
With hay! *etc.*

The boar he is a tusky beast
When great or small, when most or least,
He's welcome in at every feast,
His flesh is good, and it's well-greased

Chorus:
With hay! *etc.*

The boar's head that I bring you here,
Presents a prince without a peer,
Though he's born lowly everywhere
Yet he's a crest for knights to bear.

Chorus:
With hay! *etc.*

You lords, and knights, and young squires,
You parsons, priests, and old friars,
The boar's head is all men's desires—
And women? they, are always liars.

Chorus:
With hay! etc.

The boar's proud head, I well daresay,
Will take his leave and slip away
When he's been up till the Twelfth Day,
Then every grunt becomes a neigh.

Chorus:
With hay! *etc.*

Be glad, all, now you've seen and heard
The bearing of this brawny lord,
The boar's head, high! and hot mustard,
And may he serve as he is served.

Chorus:
With hay! *etc.*

The Early English Carols
No. 141 (Modernized English)

Chorus:
Now have good day, now have good day!
I am Christmas, and now I go my way.

Here have I dwelled with more and less
From Hallowtide to Candlemas,
And now must I from you hence pass;
Now have good-day!

I take my leave of king and knight,
And earl, baron, and lady bright;
To the wilderness I must depart;
Now have good-day.

And of the good lord of this hall
I take my leave, and of guests all;
Methinks I hear Lent doth call
Now have good-day!

And of every worthy retainer,
Marshall, pantler, and butler,
I take my leave, as for this year;
Now have good-day!

Another year I trust I shall
Make merry in this hall,
If rest and peace in England fall
Now have good-day!

But oftentimes I have heard say
That he is loath to part away
That often biddeth 'Have good-day!'
Now have good-day!

Now fare ye well, altogether;
Now fare ye well for all this year;
Yet for my sake make good cheer;
Now have good-day!

This carol is the pair to 'Welcome Yule'. It's just been hastily christened—'I am Christmas...'—and bewildered with Candlemas. But it's Yule, leaving the hall, after the Twelve Days.

His words have become old-fashioned. With no tune, how could they be sung and constantly renewed? But once they're made contemporary, they can speak to contemporary music-makers. A friend composed a tune once the words were clear.

For they don't speak only of the past. They speak of the present. We still have those who keep saying 'Good-bye' and don't go. We still have a reluctance to take down the decorations from tree and room.

Another year I trust he will
Make merry at your festival.

Now he has a tune, when two or three are gathered together, singing this carol, there will Yule be, in the midst of them.

Good Old Yule
(Restored)

Here have I stayed with everyone
Till now the New Year's just begun,
And now's the time I must be gone,
And so I'll say Good-bye.

Chorus:
Now say Good-bye, now say Good-bye,
To good old Yule, now say Good-bye.

I take my leave of men of might,
Of young, and old, and ladies bright,
Into the wilderness take flight,
And so I'll say Good-bye.

Chorus:
Now say Good-bye *etc.*

I take my leave of this room-full
Of drinking, talking, glad people.
I think I hear lean Lent-time call,
And so I'll say Good-bye.

Chorus:
Now say Good-bye *etc.*

Another year I trust I shall
Make merry at this festival,
If love and warmth do still prevail,
And so I'll say Good-bye.

Chorus:
Now say Good-bye *etc.*

But often I have heard men say
That he is loath to go away
Who says Good-bye, but still doth stay,
And so I'll say Good-bye.

Chorus:
Now say Good-bye *etc.*

Now Fare-you-well, altogether,
Now Fare-you-well, the coming year,
Now Fare-you-well, keep yet good cheer,
And so I'll say Good-bye.

Chorus:
Now say Good-bye, now say Good-bye,
To good old Yule, now say Good-bye.

GOOD OLD YULE

© 1977
Words by Norman Iles
Music by Chris Howse

Here have I stayed with ev-ry one Till

now the New Year's just be- gun And now's the

time I must be gone And so I'll say Good-

bye Now say Good- bye, now say Good- bye

To Good Old Yule Now say Good- bye

209

I Saw Three Ships

(Current Version)

I saw three ships come sailing in,
Chorus: On Christmas Day, on Christmas Day,
I saw three ships come sailing in
Chorus: On Christmas Day in the morning.

And what was in those ships all three?
Chorus: On Christmas Day, on Christmas Day,
And what was in those ships all three?
Chorus: On Christmas Day in the morning.

3: Our Saviour Christ and his lady,
On Christmas Day, on Christmas Day,
Our Saviour Christ and his lady
On Christmas Day in the morning.

4: Pray, whither sailed those ships all three?

5: O, they sailed into Bethlehem.

6: And all the bells on earth shall ring,

7: And all the angels in heaven shall sing,

8: And all the souls on earth shall sing,

9: Then let us all rejoice amain!

OTHER VERSIONS:

Sunny Bank

As I sat on a sunny bank, a sunny bank, a sunny bank,
As I sat on a sunny bank
On Christmas Day in the morning.

I spied three ships come sailing by, come sailing by,
    come sailing by,
I spied three ships come sailing by,
On Christmas Day in the morning.

3. And who should be with those three ships
   But Joseph and his fair lady!

4. O he did whistle, and she did sing,
   On Christmas Day in the morning.

5. And all the bells on earth did ring
   On Christmas Day in the morning.

6. For joy that our Saviour he was born,
   On Christmas Day in the morning.

As I Sat by My Old Cottage Door

As I sat by my old cottage door,
Old cottage door, old cottage door,
As I sat by my old cottage door
On Christmas Day in the morning.

2. I saw three ships come sailing by

3. I asked what they had got in them

4. They said they'd got their Saviour there

5. I asked them where they were taking Him to

6.   They said they took him to Jerusalem

7. I asked what they would do with Him there

8. They said that they would Him crucify

No. 471 Oxford Dictionary of Nursery Rhymes

I saw three ships come sailing by,
Come sailing by, come sailing by,
I saw three ships come sailing by,
On New Year's day in the morning.

And what do you think was in them then,
Was in them then, was in them then?
And what do you think was in them then
On New Year's day in the morning?

Three pretty girls were in them then,
Were in them then, were in them then,
Three pretty girls were in them then,
On New Year's day in the morning.

One could whistle, and one could sing,
And one could play on the violin;
Such joy there was at my wedding,
On New Year's day in the morning.

'And what was in those ships all three?' 'Our Saviour Christ and his lady.' How can two people be in three ships? Baby and mother would surely be together in one ship, so what was in the other two?

'Pray, whither sailed those ships all three?' 'O, they sailed to Bethlehem.' But there is no port at Bethlehem. Can the answer mean that Jesus is going to Bethlehem to be born? No, that won't fit either. If the ships are some sort of womb-image, Mary herself would not be part of their burden. Why ask 'Whither?' at all, when the singer has already said he saw them come sailing in?

So the next two questions get answers that do not answer. Then the carol goes on for four more verses with rejoicings only: 'And all the bells on earth shall ring', 'And all the angels in heaven shall sing', 'And all the souls on earth shall sing', 'Then let us all rejoice amain'. Did folk really compose something as repetitive as that? Odd that they should so run out of invention, when they've just imagined the three ships and begun to ask original questions!

For there is no Bible story about three ships. So folk who had pictured something entirely new, suddenly, in verses 6, 7, 8 and 9, cannot go on with their own invention. Either that or their composition was taken over by a monk and given very short shrift. That quick take-over is confirmed by the change in rhyme. Verses 2, 3 and 4 rhyme in 'ee'. Verses 6, 7 and 8 rhyme in 'ing'. Verse 9 doesn't rhyme at all.

The other two versions show that there were, indeed, further verses which did carry on the imagery. From consideration of them, we can return to the original folk-song before it was pirated. The one in the *Oxford Dictionary of Nursery Rhymes* shows that there is a folk-source for the song. From it, the words descended to the nursery.

But first let us consider the 'Sunny Bank'. I like that

picture of sunniness at the turn of the year. That is what the rejoicing was basically about. The three ships 'sailing by' must be right because then the question 'Whither?' may be put. In the ships are 'Joseph and his fair lady . . . O, he did whistle and she did sing.' Although I couldn't make much of those actions, I noted that this Joseph and Mary are far from their Biblical characters. Maybe they were other people, whose names had been changed?

I made more of that version that hides among the nursery rhymes.

Three pretty girls were in them then . . .
One could whistle and one could sing,
And one could play on the violin . . .
Such joy there was at my wedding,
On New Year's day in the morning.

For the first time, the number fits. Three pretty girls. And the rejoicings are given a cause, the wedding, that fits them. Not only does the number fit, but the cargo fits the means of transport! Sailing ships, with swelling sails, have always been referred to as 'she'. They can rightly carry girls. This is a cargo of happiness. Hence the rejoicing. 'When my ship comes in' is still a folk-saying.

Also the 'New Year's day' suggests that this is the least altered version. As soon as any Christian got hold of an old pagan song about the New Year festival, the first and easiest alteration he made was to put 'Christmas Day' (with a capital D) in place of New Year's day.

But I think it has suffered some alteration, perhaps forgetting, at the end. To have three ships, bringing three playing, singing, dancing (?) girls to 'my wedding' is too personal and too small a conclusion for all these preliminaries. What is needed is a cause of general rejoicing—two of the Christian versions have the nativity, while the third has the crucifixion, which is, doubtless, part of the Christian paradox. However, 'my wedding' does not make everyone rejoice amain. But if we're all to get a pretty girl each, we might all whistle, sing or even play on the violin! The girls would be types, not individuals, for three is a very prime, very typical, number. It derives its significance from the three sexual parts of man and woman. Hence the saying 'All good things come in threes', 'Three's a lot', even 'Three bags full'. The three ships themselves are three because of the sexual significance of the number.

If this argosy of beautiful women is sailing by, men will ask whither they are sailing. Then, as they—and we—are told they are sailing in, there will be general rejoicing.

When? On New Year's Day in the morning. That 'in the morning' does have significance. At cock-crow.

The rest is a matter of form. The question and answer dialogue must be continued throughout the song, as it is (in reported speech) in 'As I Sat by My Old Cottage Door'. The 'I' is the man coast-watcher. The chorus, who ask the questions, are the land-sailors. Question and answer should—if possible!—rhyme.

I Saw Three Ships (Restored)

Solo Man:
As I sat on a sunny bank
On New Year's Day, on New Year's Day,
As I sat on a sunny bank
I saw a sight of joy in the morning.

Chorus:
What saw you for a sight of joy?
On New Year's Day, on New Year's Day,
What saw you for a sight of joy?
On New Year's Day in the morning.

Solo Man:
I saw three ships come sailing by
On New Year's Day, on New Year's Day,
I saw three ships come sailing by
On New Year's Day in the morning.

Chorus:
And how came by those ships all three?
On New Year's Day, on New Year's Day,
And how came by those ships all three?
On New Year's Day in the morning.

Solo Man:
With rounded sail and ribbons free,
On New Year's Day, on New Year's Day,
With rounded sail and ribbons free,
On New Year's Day in the morning.

Chorus:
And what was in those ships all three?
On New Year's Day, on New Year's Day,
And what was in those ships all three?
On New Year's Day in the morning.

Solo Man:
'Twas girl, and wife, and gay lady,
On New Year's Day, on New Year's Day,
'Twas girl, and wife, and gay lady,
On New Year's Day in the morning.

Chorus:
And whither sailed those ships all three?
On New Year's Day, on New Year's Day,
And whither sailed those ships all three?
On New Year's Day in the morning.

Solo Man:
They sailed to us this very way,
On New Year's Day, on New Year's Day,
They sailed to us this very way,
On New Year's Day in the morning.

Chorus:
Then let us give such shipping thank!
On New Year's Day, on New Year's Day,
Then let us give such shipping thank!
On New Year's Day in the morning.

The Greensleeves Carol

(Current Version)

The old year now away is fled,
The new year it is entered,
Then let us now our sins down-tread
And joyfully all appear.
Let's merry be this day,
And let us now both sport and play,
Hang grief, cast care away!
God send you a happy New Year!

The name day now of Christ we keep
Who for our sins did often weep;
His hands and feet were wounded deep
And his blessed side with a spear.
His head they crowned with thorn,
And at him they did laugh and scorn,
Who for our good was born;
God send us a happy New Year!

And now with New Year's gifts each friend
Unto each other they do send;
God grant we may all our lives amend
And that the truth may appear.
Now like the snake your skin
Cast off, of evil thoughts and sin,
And so the year begin;
God send us a happy New Year!

That it should come to this! That lovely tune—the carol still keeping its name—all spoiled by the sins, and the grief, and the evil thoughts.

I agree with two sentiments in the carol. I like to be merry. I like the truth to appear. I determined to restore the truth and, in so doing, the merriment.

218

The beginning is right. That tells what we are singing about, nothing other than the coming of the New Year. But then some Churchman has to put in his word 'sins'. Praising the New Year has nothing to do with sin. It's a natural rejoicing, pure 'merriness' as the wassailers would call it.

That second verse demonstrates how the whole theme of a carol can be twisted. From the given subject of the first verse, we are misled into the 'name day of Christ' and to his crucifixion! But how are we to be merry, 'Hang grief, cast care away', if we are to think of 'His hands and feet were wounded deep, And his blessed side with a spear'? Further, even in the Church's calendar, that subject is for Easter, not Christmas. Here any reader can see the monk caught black-handed.

In verse 3 we return to the original subject, the New Year and its customs. Briefly. For lines 3 and 4 resume the indoctrination: 'God grant we may all our lives amend.' Then a last glimpse of the original song. That snake, who has to cast off his skin, is pre-Christian. For he is, here, an image of well-doing. Whereas he should be the tempter, doing evil. This is a sign of the age of the song, for the signs of the gods of the past become the signs of the Devil of the new order. The snake, the goat, the hoof and the horns were all signs of the old gods of fertility. They became signs of the Devil of Christianity. We discover the snake to be one of the Lords of Life, as Lawrence believed. It was partly the revival of spirit that snake gave me that energized me to his defence in prose, and to repair his song.

I joined the original rejoicers. How important that is, for the correct restoration of the song! For if you are opposed to the spirit of the song, as the monk was, you get the tone wrong—as well! In the last verse he begins to teach from outside the singers, no longer one of them. He changes from 'our' to 'your'—'Now like the snake *your* skin cast off Of evil thoughts and sin'. There is, most obviously, the voice of the teacher, not the voice of the class. God grant we may our carols amend and that the truth may appear!

The Greensleeves Carol (Restored)

The Old Year now away has fled,
The New Year it has enteréd,
Then let us now our fears down-tread
And joyfully all appear-a.
Let's merry be this day,
And let's together sport and play,
Kiss, love, cast care away,
To welcome in the New Year.

The first day of the year we keep
When we will never want nor weep,
For we have now a joy so deep
We'll show a merry cheer-a.
Houses, now, are crowned with thorn,
With berry, and with ivy-corn,
We'll fill the Wassail horn
To welcome in the New Year.

And now with New Year gifts each friend
His greeting does to other send,
So helping hands we'll ever lend
And spare not of our gear-a.
Like a snake we'll cast our skin,
And to fresh fellow-feelings win;
Living so, we shall begin
To welcome in the New Year.

The Somerset Wassail
(Current Version)

1:    Wassail, and wassail, all over the town!
       The cup it is white and the ale it is brown;
       The cup it is made of the good ashen tree,
       And so is the malt of the best barley:

       Chorus:
       For it's your wassail, and it's our wassail!
       And it's joy be to you, and a jolly wassail!

2:    O master and missus, are you all within?
       Pray open the door and let us come in:
       O master and missus a-sitting by the fire,
       Pray think upon poor trav'llers, a-trav'lling in
          the mire:

       For it's your wassail *etc.*

3:    O where is the maid, with the silver-headed pin,
       To open the door, and let us come in?
       O master and missus, it is our desire
       A good loaf and cheese, and a toast by the fire:

       For it's your wassail *etc.*

4:    There was an old man, and he had an old cow,
       And how for to keep her he didn't know how,
       He built up a barn for to keep his cow warm,
       And a drop or two of cider will do us no harm:

       No harm, boys, harm: no harm, boys, harm:
       And a drop or two of cider will do us no harm.

5:   The girt dog of Langport he burnt his long tail,
       And this is the night we go singing wassail:
       O master and missus, now we must be gone;
       God bless all in this house till we do come again:

For it's your wassail *etc.**

Is that trembling cry a song? Can it be a song of joy? A wassail reduced to misery, fed with cold and usurous hand! Blake would have called it a wassail of bitter experience. All it can do is apologize for itself and beg bread and cheese from master and missus.

Can it have its Infant Joy restored? The fighting spirit of the Norse farmers revived?

The clue is that the second halves of the verses don't join on to the first halves. Those second halves are second thoughts. They're the result of the poverty and humiliation the farm labourers have endured. They ask to come in, and then they have to humble themselves, in case they've been too bold: 'Pray think upon poor travellers, a-travelling in the mire.' They ask where the maid is but don't follow up their question. Instead, they ask for bread and cheese. They beg the question. They begin to tell about a man and a cow. Then they withdraw into the safety of a 'drop or two of cider'. Their chorus becomes 'No harm'. They're apologizing in advance. The great dog of Langport is mentioned, how he burnt his long tail, but the story isn't continued. Instead, 'We must be gone'. So is the jollity from the so-called 'Jolly wassail'.

It's only the labourers, or the landless men, the travellers in the mire, who have kept up the old tradition. The farmers are dropping it. No more are equals singing to equals. In this special case they were singing to Cecil Sharp, who looked alien to them. So

(*Collected by Cecil Sharp in 1908.)

no more is it 'Your wassail and our wassail'.

Wassail jollity was not Victorian gentility. 'Wassail' meant 'Be healthy' and 'Be fertile, be happy', for people, animals and apple-trees were all wassailed. But gentility meant 'Be respectable'. So this is not the Somerset Wassail. It's the Victorian version of the original song.

How do we restore it? By following the sense of the first halves of the verses.

The 'no harm' gives a clue. They are frightened of the effect of what they might be singing, though they haven't sung it! The missing halves could be taken amiss by their employers, who may still know them but don't sing them.

The beginnings of verses 4 and 5 are the clearest examples of 'fertile' beginnings. The old man who doesn't know how to keep a cow ... Is there anyone who doesn't know how to keep a cow? In those days? And is this jolly wassail really about dairy-farming with one cow? Is the old man an agéd man? We're being too literal. This familiar man is ignorant of a different sort of husbandry: wife-keeping. 'Cow' cannot have been so derogatory then as it is now. The censored last line can be deduced. It must tell how he did manage to keep her—that is, to keep her from running-off. It even gives a clue to his method. It must be something to do with keeping her warm.

The girt dog of Langport has a long tail. He's big and he's long. His tail stands up. He burnt it. How? That's the censored point. Some gay dog must have burnt it trying to keep a cow warm!

However, I see that Cecil Sharp, the great Victorian who collected the wassail, thought the dog was a reference to the Danes, 'whose invasion of Langport is not yet forgotten in that town'. Let's think that explanation over for a moment. Does the great dog fit a Danish invasion? Was that invasion on 'the night we go singing wassail'? If the explanation does not fit, it tells us a lot about Sharp's bias in favour of irrelevant scholarship. I can tell you a lot about my bias by saying I think the dog was a Great Dane.

If verses 4 and 5 are sexual, then the chance of verses 2 and 3 being jolly on the same subject should put new light into our eyes as we re-read about the master and missus sitting by the fire, and the maid with the silver-headed pin. These verses aren't as warm as the later ones, because 'no harm' doesn't occur till after them. To begin, we're only well-wishing the chilly old folks, then their well-endowed, unmarried daughter.

Now, if we can decide whether it's cider we're drinking (as in verse 4) or 'malt of the best barley' (verse 1); whether we're drinking it out of a 'cup' or a proper wassail-bowl; whether we want to sing the 'no harm' chorus as well as the 'jolly wassail' one; and whether our last verse isn't really two verses compressed into one, we'll restore the wassail in the right way.

I don't say the only way. I am guided by the beginnings. But my aim is not sharp! There will be different endings. But they will not be very different. Any way of keeping the cow warm will do. Any way of awakening the daughter. Place-names will be changed. Langport will be any place, any port, known for randy men. Cider will change to beer. The wassail was not limited to one county just because it was collected there. It came from Norway.

The great realization is that the song's been half buried. But it can be freed from the earth, from the corruptions, and move again. A song is a man singing. This one is calling, 'And it's joy be to you, and a jolly wassail.'

The Warm Wassail
(Restored)

1:   Wassail! and Wassail! all over the town,
      Our bowl it is white and our cider is brown,
      Our bowl it is made of the good apple tree,
      And our cider inside 'er's as strong as can be.

      Chorus:
      For it's your Wassail, and it's our Wassail,
      And all joy be to you with this jolly Wassail.

2:   O neighbours and friends, are you now all within?
      Pray open the door and let us come in,
      O neighbours and friends, sitting down by the fire,
      May your fire burn longer, and higher and higher!

      Chorus:
      For it's your Wassail *etc.*

3:   O where is the maid with the silver-headed pin,
      To open the door and with us to sing?
      To her and all women it is our desire
      To give as warm greeting as they can require!

      Chorus:
      For it's your Wassail *etc.*

4:   There was an old man and he had an old cow,
      To keep and provend 'er he did not know how,
      He built her a barn for to keep her so warm,
      And then he did warm her from night until morn!

      Chorus:
      For it's your Wassail *etc.*

5: The girt dog of Devonport he burnt his long tail,
    And this is the night he goes singing wassail,
    He lies at our feet, and he stands at our front,
    And this is the night that he comes out to hunt!

    Chorus:
    For it's your Wassail *etc.*

6: O neighbours and friends, we must now be gone,
    Bless all in this house 'till we do come again,
    May all of you be happy, and have all that you want,
    And your troubles be little, and laid at the font!

    Chorus:
    For it's your Wassail, and it's our Wassail
    And all joy be to you with this jolly Wassail.

Spring Carols

I Sing of a Maiden
(Restored: Tune—parts of 'Au clair de la lune')

Solo man:
I sing of a maiden
All alone was she,
For her joy and comfort
A stranger soon chose she.

He came to her silently
Where this maiden was,
Silently as dew falls
On the April grass.

He came to her secretly
To this maiden's bower,
Secretly as dew falls
On the April flower.

He came to her stealthily
Where this maiden lay,
Stealthily as dew falls
On the April spray.

I sing of a maiden
All alone was she,
Well may such a maiden
All our mothers be!

Let us imagine we are fifteenth century monks who have determined to church this ballad, which is very popular, alas, with the peasants.

The maiden will obviously be Mary. 'All alone was she' is easy. We begin: 'I sing of a maiden That was without a mate' ('make-less' in our English) She can't choose a stranger to comfort her, not even the Holy

Ghost, for Scripture says she, herself, was chosen. The only person we can say she chose is Jesus, and that will account for her being pregnant in the last verse, so we have the sense of 'She chose Jesus for her son', and a line to spare, because we dropped 'For her joy and comfort'. We want to impress the people, the nobility and even the king that this baby she chooses is—or ought to be—in command of them. We've had trouble with the Henrys. So our next two lines are

The King of all Kings
She chose for her son.

We like the 'all'. It's just a pity that those lines don't follow the sense of 'without a mate'.

Now, the next three verses. No need to change much at all. We'll put 'mother' for 'maiden', and we'll go on

He came to her silently
Where his mother was,
Silently as dew falls
On the April grass.

He came to her secretly
To his mother's bower,
Secretly as dew falls
On the April flower.

He came to her stealthily
Where his mother lay,
Stealthily as dew falls
On the April spray.

So far, I think you'll agree, we haven't worked very hard. Unfortunately, we've left in April, the spring month, and that ripening progression of 'grass', 'flower' and 'spray' that goes with 'was', 'bower', and 'lay'. We do wonder about 'Where his mother lay', and the dew might still awaken associations with spring fertility in some peasant head. It's a pity there's nothing in the Bible about April, or Mary lying down. But it could be tradition, couldn't it?

After dinner, the last verse makes us think a bit. In affirmatory mood, and to deny peasants their joke, we begin

Mother and maiden
Was never none but she.

That ought to stop them! And then we see that we need only alter the ballad's last line. So down we put on our parchment:

Well may such a maiden
God's mother be.

The 'may' is still wrong. But what a flash of inspiration! What affirmation of our faith is in our 'Well'!

After the passage of time has worsened our version, this will become carol 183 in the *Oxford Book of Carols*. As you peasants won't all have it to hand, I'll quote it. You will be gratified to learn that Professor Saintsbury will write: 'In no previous verse had this Aeolian music—this "harp of Ariel"—that distinguishes English at its very best in this direction . . . been given to the world.' So someone thought we did a good job.

I Sing of a Maiden

(Current Version)

I sing of a maiden
That is *make-less;*   [matchless, *Oxford Book of Carols*;
                          mate-less *NCI*]
King of all kings
To her son she *ches.*   [chose]

He came all so still
Where his mother was,
As dew in April
That falleth on the grass.

He came all so still
To his mother's bower,
As dew in April
That falleth on the flower.

He came all so still
Where his mother lay,
As dew in April
That falleth on the spray.

Mother and maiden
Was never none but she;
Well may such a lady
Godes mother be.

The Furry Day Carol
(Current Version)

1: Remember us poor Mayers all!
    And thus we do begin-a,
    To lead our lives in righteousness,
    Or else we die in sin-a:

    Chorus:
    With Holanto, Holanto,
    Holanto, sing merry,
    With Holanto, sing merry-O,
    With Holanto, sing merry!

2: We have been rambling half the night,
    And almost all the day-a,
    And now, returned back again,
    We've brought you a branch of May-a:

    With Holanto *etc.*

3: O, we were up as soon as day,
    To fetch the summer home-a;
    The summer is a-coming on,
    And winter is a gone-a:

    With Holanto *etc.*

4: Then let us all most merry be,
    And sing with cheerful voice-a;
    For we have good occasion now
    This time for to rejoice-a.

    With Holanto *etc.*

5: St. George he next shall be our song:
    St. George he was a knight-a;
    Of all the men in Christendom
    St. George he was the right-a

    With Holanto *etc.*

6: God bless our land with power and might,
    God send us peace in England:
    Pray send us peace both day and night,
    For ever in merry England.

    With Holanto *etc.*

Poor Mayers-all! They were forced to sing:

To lead our lives in righteousness
Or else we die in sin-a.

All they wanted to do was die in sin! The merriment they longed for would be called sin by whoever changed the words.

He didn't put much doctrine in. There's just the mention of Christendom and peace. But he took all the merriness out! With every chorus calling for it, no verse has it. A thorough Christian gentleman. Our task is to restore the original sin version, the merriment that was May Morning.

It's the kind of merriment that went with the Horse-play. Still, the May Day Horse ducks his head under women's skirts. It's the kind of merriment that went with the maypole. Still, young people dance round the phallic symbol, with ribbons on. And it's the kind of merriment that went with gathering the May boughs in the woods at dawn. Still 'Many a green gown is given'—if not at dawn, then at dusk.

At Padstow, on May morning, they still sing 'Unite,

and unite, and let us all unite.' All, but in pairs.

The celibate was trying to make Nature conform to celibacy. The May was not for him. It was, it is, for hawthorn berries, for hips.

His first verse is so absolutely against the meaning of May that an absolute opposite must have been there. The priest must have heard something like:

Remember us, glad Mayers all,
For thus we do begin-a
To lead our lives in happiness
Or else we'll not live at all-a!

Black has become white. The May is beginning to blossom.

Where do we go from there? Into the chorus. And the chorus isn't going anywhere. 'Sing merry' three times, but nothing to sing merry about. 'Holanto' is meaningless. Even if it meant 'Heel and toe', that wouldn't move us.

The word 'thus' tells us that there was some other word in Holanto's place, a word that told us *how* the Mayers were going to begin, and go on, all their lives through. Not with 'Heel and toe'. With weaving in and out.

Verse 2 has 'Rambling half the night/And almost all the day-a'. That's wrong. The Mayers don't ramble all the day-a. They bring the May boughs back early in the morning. 'And now returned back again.' They were doing something else half the morn-a. Even 'gambolling half the morn-a' would give some idea of what they'd been up to.

The branch of May they're bringing back is more than a pretty spray of blossom. 'It is but a sprout but it's well budded-out', as another May song sings. It's a symbol. Ever smelled it? It's the prickly holly of the spring.

Verse 3 has not a twinkle left in it. Any fool could sing it. No one else would want to. The form tells us where the joke was. In the second two lines. For in those the repetition shows the rewriting.

But the repetition doesn't rhyme. The joke rhymed with 'home'. The spirits of the dead Mayers will accept any joke as right. What they will not accept is no joke at all. Once we realize the tone of the song, we may mow our meads and our maids, and make the song into a folk-song again.

'Then let us all most merry be'—and take out 'good occasion' in verse 4. You can tell the new language, as well as the new religion. There was a 'good chance' on May morning of making love. That makes us rejoice-a.

'St George he was a knight-a.' What a statement of the known! Did the simple peasants really sing something as simple as that? And follow it with 'St George he was the right-a'? Then they must have been village idiots. St George was the kind of knight folk meànt when they said, oh, so simply, 'Once a king always a king. But once a knight is enough for any man.' (That is why the papal commission could not find any historical evidence for St George.) Our patron saint was the Cerne Abbas giant in armour. He was right, because he was always up-right! He was the paternal saint of England.

In case you think I'm being too phallic, remember the Maypole. That's a good lance.

The converter gets straight in to the last verse with his 'God bless'. The sense, though is 'St. George bless'. And though peace is very nice, these Mayers aren't pacifists at this moment. Doubtless they'd all be supporters of the Campaign for Nuclear Disarmament, but they're not thinking about that when they've got flowers in their hats and bells on their legs. They would not sing, at that time, 'Send peace by day and night'. For that's overdoing it. Send something else by day and night. Night begins to sound significant, instead of insignificant. 'Send love by day and night.'

God is love. It just depends on the kind of love you mean. The Mayers are singing about May love. Their song must be furrier all the way through—and funnier, too. Then, it will fit 'The sap is rising.'

The May-Pluckers' Carol (Restored)

1: Come, join with us, May-pluckers all,
   For thus we do begin-O,
   To lead our lives to summer-time
   Or else it comes not in-O!

   Chorus:
   With to and fro, sing merry-berry-O!
   With to and fro, sing merry!
   With to and fro, sing merry-berry-O!
   With to and fro, sing merry!

2: We have been rambling half the night,
   And dandling half the morn-O,
   And now we're rantling back again
   To bear the flower and thorn-O!

   With to and fro *etc.*

3: O we were up before the day
   To fetch the summer home-O,
   Now summer we have brought it home,
   And winter's made 'ls moan-O!

   With to and fro *etc.*

4: Then let us all most merry, merry be,
    And sing with lusty voice-O,
    And we will have a chance or two
    This morning to rejoice-O!

    With to and fro *etc.*

5: Saint George shall next be in our song,
    Saint George he is our knight-O,
    Of all the knights in all the year
    This knight is always upright-O!

    With to and fro *etc.*

6: Saint George send now his right and might,
    Saint George send power to upstand-O,
    May maids bloom white by day and night,
    Saint George for merry England-O!

    With to and fro, sing merry-berry-O!
    With to and fro, sing merry!
    With to and fro, sing merry-berry-O!
    With to and fro, sing merry!

Good King Wenceslas or Tempus Adest Floridum

(Current Version)

1: Spring has now unwrapped the flowers,
   Day is fast reviving,
   Life in all her growing powers
   Towards the light is striving:
   Gone the iron touch of cold,
   Winter time and frost time,
   Seedlings, working through the mould,
   Now make up for lost time.

2: Herb and plant that, winter long,
   Slumbered at their leisure,
   Now bestirring, green and strong,
   Find in growth their pleasure:
   All the world with beauty fills,
   Gold the green enhancing;
   Flowers make glee among the hills,
   And set the meadows dancing.

3: Through each wonder of fair days
   God himself expresses;
   Beauty follows all his ways,
   As the world he blesses:
   So, as he renews the earth,
   Artist without rival,
   In his grace of glad new birth
   We must seek revival.

4: Earth put on her dress of glee;
   Flowers and grasses hide her;
   We go forth in charity—
   Brothers all, beside her;
   For, as man this glory sees
   In the awakening season,
   Reason learns the heart's decrees,
   And hearts are led by reason.

5: Praise the Maker, all ye saints;
   He with glory girt you,
   He who skies and meadows paints
   Fashioned all your virtue;
   Praise him, seers, heroes, kings,
   Heralds of perfection;
   Brothers, praise him, for he brings
   All to resurrection!*

OTHER VERSIONS:

The original Latin words are:

Tempus adest floridum, surgunt namque flores
Vernales in omnibus imitantur mores,
Hoc, quod frigus laeserat, reparant calores,
Cernimus hoc fieri per multos labores.

Sunt prata plena floribus jucanda aspectu,
Ubi juvat herbas cum delectua,
Gramina plantae (quae) hyeme quiescunt,
Vernali in tempore virent accrescunt.

Haec vobis pulchre monstrant Deum Creatore,
Quem quoque nos credimus omnium factorem:
O tempus ergo hilare, quo laetari libet,
Renovato nam mundo, no novari decet.

*From The *Oxford Book of Carols* by permission of Oxford University Press.

Terra ornatur floribus multo decore,
Nos honestis moribus vero amore,
Gaudeamus igitur tempore jucundo,
Laudemusque Dominum pectoris ex fundo.

The reader may be surprised to see the title 'Good King Wenceslas'. It is there because the foot-note to that carol, in the *Oxford Book of Carols,* says 'This [Good King Wenceslas] owes its popularity to the delightful tune, which is that of the Spring Carol, *"Tempus Adest Floridum"* Unfortunately, Neale, in 1863, substituted [it] for the Spring Carol.'

So here is an acknowledged substitution, done as late as 1863. A Christian indoctrinator took the tune from an old carol but completely rewrote its words. Why? He would never have done that if the original words, no matter how poor poetically, were Christian. A glance at *'Tempus Adest Floridum'* shows how doctrine-free, how natural, its beginning was. Further, if we had only the substitution, no restoration would be logically possible. The tune, too, would be taken over, and 'Good King Wenceslas' would be a sacred hymn, untouchable by any doubter.

'Tempus Adest Floridum' itself is one of a collection made in 1582 by Theodoricus Petrus of Finnish and Swedish carols. He called the songs *Piae Cantones,* and they spread through the reformed Church of Sweden and Finland. 'An edition of his work (altered) was published in 1910' (information from the foot-note to No. 141, *Oxford Book of Carols*).

Folk-songs about Spring collected before 1582 must have been secular or pagan, for Christianity has no Spring carols. The celebration of the seasons of the year, Christmas, Easter, Harvest Festival, are all pagan in origin. Easter itself is sacred to Eastea, the Anglo-Saxon goddess of Spring. In Scandinavia she will have had a different name but been even more honoured.

So this Protestant devotee collected Natural songs and called them 'Pious'. He shows his intention with that title. How far his purpose was from 'Spring has now unwrapped the flowers, Day is fast reviving'! How far his Latin education is taking him from the vernacular. He has even re-written his own name!

Luckily he was an even quicker adapter than Friar Ryman. For his *'Tempus Adest Floridum'* is not deeply indoctrinated, not deeply indoctrinated enough! Only verses 3 and 4 have passing mentions of God.

This did not please. Neale rejected his version, and the editor of the *OBC* doctored it more strongly. The footnote to his version says 'This is a free translation, with a doxology . . . '. What did he mean by a 'free translation'? He meant

Reason learns the heart's decrees,
And hearts are led by reason

is his version of

Gaudeamus igitur tempore jucundo
Laudemusque Dominum pectoris ex fundo
Which, in my English, is

Let us be joyful, therefore, in the happy time
And let us praise God from the bottom of our hearts.

What did he mean by 'with a doxology'? He meant 'with a hymn ascribing glory to God' (Chambers' *Dictionary*). He meant, 'I've added the whole of verse 5 without any justification whatsoever.'

What does a restorer do? Drop verse 5? Yes, I did. But I then found that the preceding verses do not conclude. They do need another verse. So the question becomes, what is a fitting one? Is it a doxology? Or is it some general conclusion about Spring? Let everyone follow his heart's 'reason'!

Good King Spring at Last (Restored: Tune—'Good King Wenceslas')

1: Spring has now unfolded flowers
     Sun is fast reviving,
     Life with all its growing powers
     Towards the light is striving.
     Gone the iron touch of cold,
     Winter-time and frost-time,
     Seedlings working through the mould
     Now push up to Spring-time.

2: Shoot and bud that winter-long
     Slumbered in the earth, bare,
     Now bestirring green and strong,
     Find in growth their pleasure.
     All the world with beauty fills,
     Gold with green advancing,
     Flowers make joy among the hills,
     Set the meadows dancing.

*4: Earth puts on her shining dress,
     Flowers and grasses grace her,
     We go forth with happiness
     In companies beside her;
     For as we this greenness see
     In the 'wakening season,
     So we learn the heart's decree,
     Hearts are led by feeling!

* I omitted verse 3.

5: Wandering onwards in a band,
    Pairing as the birds do,
    Lad and lass go hand in hand,
    Song is in each heart, too;
    Love shoots up in glad glancings,
    Flowering this season,
    Praise the Spring-time for it brings
    All to exaltation!

A New Dial

(Current Version)

In those twelve days let us be glad, in those
twelve days let us be glad,
For God of his power hath all things made.

What are they that are but one? What are
they that are but one?
One God, one Baptism, and one Faith,
One Truth there is, the scripture saith:

What are they that are but two? What are they
that are but two?
Two Testaments, the old and new,
We do acknowledge to be true:

[The other verses follow this pattern, so I give the
answers only.]

Three Persons are in Trinity
Which makes one God in unity:

Four sweet Evangelists there are,
Christ's birth, life, death, which do declare:

Five senses, like five kings, maintain
In every man a several reign:

Six days to labour is not wrong,
For God himself did work so long:

Seven liberal arts hath God sent down
With divine skill man's soul to crown:

Eight beatitudes are there given;
Use them aright and go to heaven:

Nine Muses, like the heaven's nine spheres,
With sacred tunes entice our ears:

Ten Statutes God to Moses gave,
Which, kept or broke, do spill or save:

Eleven thousand Virgins did partake,
And suffered death for Jesus' sake:

Twelve are attending on God's son;
Twelve make our Creed. The dial's done:

OTHER VERSIONS:

Green Grow the Rushes-O!

I'll sing you one-O!
Green grow the rushes-O!
What is your one-O?
One is one and all alone,
And ever more shall be so!

I'll sing you two-O!
Green grow the rushes-O!
What is your two-O?
Two, two, the lily-white boys
Clothed all in green-O,
One is one and all alone,
And ever more shall be so,

[The other verses follow this pattern,
so I give the last verse.]

I'll sing you twelve-O!
Green grow the rushes-O!
What is your twelve-O?
Twelve for the twelve apostles,
Eleven for the eleven who went to heaven,
And ten for the ten commandments,
Nine for the nine bright shiners,
Eight for the April rainers,
Seven for the seven stars in the sky,
And six for the six proud walkers,
Five for the symbols at your door,
And four for the Gospel makers,
Three, three, the rivals,
Two, two, the lily-white boys
Clothed all in green-O,
One is one and all alone,
And ever more shall be so.

It took a priest to catch a priest! I don't think I would have recognized the origin of 'A New Dial' if the Reverend Routley had not written in *The English Carol:* 'It [Green Grow the Rushes-O] stands somewhere in the background of 'A New Dial'. Alerted, I saw that numbers 4 (the Gospel Makers) 10 (Commandments) and 12 (Apostles) are the same in both songs. But the others! How completely different the songs now are! How bold, how rightly bold, the restorer would be who worked on 'A New Dial' alone. How amazed all of us would be if he produced something like 'Green Grow the Rushes-O!' out of it!

It looks as if the folk-song began to be converted by altering numbers 4, 10, 11 and 12. Then the author of 'A New Dial' went through all the rest of the numbers with his Christian substitutions.

We can put right the Christian numbers, when we understand the non-Christian ones. Once we've understood who is the one who is all alone, who the lily-white boys are and who are the rivals, we shall be able to replace the Gospel makers. The chorus is the great clue. 'Green Grow the Rushes-O!' Spring's come. The bull-rushes are green. Love's come. Consequently, all these numbers are love-lust numbers. This is a song like the modern 'Roll me over in the clover.'

'And this is number one, And the fun has just begun'—but this number one is all alone, and ever more shall be so. So he is, at first. He stands alone. He begins.

Then come the two, the lily-white boys. Who would follow him, in sexual association? There's only one pair that's 'lily-white'. The usual folk-description is 'lily-white tits and golden hair'. So 'boys' just means 'things', as guineas were called 'yellow boys', 'Clothed all in green-O!' means that they are young and perky.

Three are not the rivals. That would be only two. They are something that sounds like rivals.

Four are some kind of makers, but not Gospel makers. I remembered the saying 'It takes more than four bare buttocks in bed to make a marriage.' Agreed. But it doesn't take fewer.

'Five' are 'at your door'. I've heard the 'back door' used to describe the arse. So, to the front entrance. There must be five of something at a girl's front door.

Six are proud. What do the folk associate with six, particularly at this stage of love-making? Six inches.

The seven stars in the sky are right, but they are not now obviously right because we no longer understand they are the Plough. That was the sign of ploughing the field and scattering the good seed on the land—in full double-meaning. The Plough was a pub sign because it meant more than one kind of work.

Eight for the April rainers. Right again. Spring rain is part of insemination.

Nine has only one significance in folk-sexology.

Nine bright, shining, lunar months.

Once the nine months are over, the baby born, it's time to 'begin again'. As in 'Roll me over'. And therefore 11 and 12 are simply Christian additions. Somebody wanted to get the Apostles in—twice!

So the folk-song is freed from the non-understanding which has come over it. It's like a wassail, very old, from a farming community that sang about fertility. As time passed, not only was the meaningful metaphor no longer understood. The very meaning itself was thought improper and was disguised. The New Dial is very proper and very plain. Unfortunately, such a clock didn't work. It stopped. No one sang it. It has no spring! Now the real song reappears, as old and as new as the sun, and the sun-dial. It has the spring.

Green Grow the Rushes-O! (Restored)

1st Solo: I'll sing you one-O.

Chorus: Green grow the rushes-O!
What is your one-O?

1st Solo: One is One and all alone,
And ever more shall be so!

2nd Solo: I'll sing you two-O.

Chorus: Green grow the rushes-O!
What is your two-O?

2nd Solo: Two, two, the Lily-White Lambs
Clothed all in green-O!

Chorus: One is One and all alone,
And ever more shall be so!

3rd Solo: I'll sing you three-O.

Chorus: Green grow the rushes-O!
What is your three-O?

3rd Solo: Three, three, the Ribalds!

Chorus: Two, two, the Lily-White Lambs
Clothed all in green-O;
One is One and all alone,
And ever more shall be so!

4th Solo: I'll sing you four-O.

Chorus: Green grow the rushes-O!
What is your four-O?

4th Solo: Four for the Merry Makers!

Chorus: Three, three, the Ribalds,
Two, two, the Lily-White Lambs
Clothed all in green-O;
One is One *etc.*

5th Solo: I'll sing you five-O.

Chorus: Green grow the rushes-O!
What is your five-O?
5th Solo: Five for the Fiddlers at your Door!

Chorus: And four for the Merry Makers;
Three, three, the Ribalds,
Two, two, the Lily-White Lambs *etc.*

6th Solo: I'll sing you six-O.

Chorus: Green grow the rushes-O!
What is your six-O?

6th Solo: Six for the six Proud Standers!

Chorus: Five for the Fiddlers at your Door,
And four for the Merry Makers;
Three, three, the Ribalds *etc.*

7th Solo: I'll sing you seven-O.

Chorus: Green grow the rushes-O!
What is your seven-O?

7th Solo: Seven for the Plough that's in the Sky!

Chorus: And six for the six Proud Standers;
Five for the Fiddlers at your Door *etc.*

8th Solo: I'll sing you eight-O.

Chorus: Green grow the rushes-O!
What is your eight-O?

8th Solo: Eight for the April Raining!

Chorus: Seven for the Plough that's in the Sky,
And six for the six Proud Standers *etc.*

9th Solo: I'll sing you nine-O.

Chorus: Green grow the rushes-O!
What is your nine-O?

9th Solo: Nine for the nine Bright Shining Months!

Chorus:	And eight for the April Raining:
	Seven for the Plough that's in the Sky.
	And six for the six Proud Standers *etc.*
10th Solo:	I'll sing you ten-O.
Chorus:	Green grow the rushes-O!
	What is your ten-O?
10th Solo:	Ten for the New Beginners!
Chorus:	Nine for the nine Bright Shining Months,
	And eight for the April Raining;
	Seven for the Plough that's in the Sky,
	And six for the six Proud Standers;
	Five for the Fiddlers at your Door,
	And four for the Merry Makers;
	Three, three, the Ribalds,
	Two, two, the Lily-White Lambs
	Clothed all in green-O;
	One is One and all alone,
	And ever more shall be so!

'Old England, she shall win the day.'
FOLK-SONG

Bibliography

The Early English Carols, GREENE, R. (Oxford University Press, 1977) The Introduction uncovers all the hidden history of the carols' indoctrination.

The Red Book of Ossory, ed. GREENE, R. (Blackwell, 1974) The book that is documentary evidence of love-songs being converted to Christmas Carols.

How They Lived, ed. HASSALL (Blackwell, 1962) Contains information, from contemporary sources, of pre-Reformation times.

Grotesques and Gargoyles, SHERIDAN and ROSS, (David and Charles, 1975) Photographs, with commentary, of pagan imagery still existing in churches. Incidentally, it tells where our most-unaltered, pagan churches are located.

English Inn Signs, LARWOOD and HOTTON (Blaketon Hall, 1985) The signs that people would go under, from Roman times till the present. In London there were thirty-three 'Maidenheads' in 1630. 'I was in The Maiden head last night' must have been a common cockney joke at that date.

The Silbury Treasure and *The Avebury Cycle*, DAMES, R. (Thames and Hudson, 1976, 1977) Revelation after revelation of the meaning and use of our great, pagan monuments. Silbury Mound is the earth's womb. The monuments, including Stonehenge, were used to link earth's seasons to man's.

Primitive Erotic Art, ed RAWSON, P. (Weidenfeld and Nicholson, 1973) The only scholarly book I know that understands the symbolism of people's art.

Aku, Aku, Heyerdahl, T. (Penguin, 1960) Thor Heyerdahl finds the pagan gods on Easter Island still

252

being reverenced, underground; and traces someone who knew the old way of erecting the enormous stone heads.

Folk Song in Britain, LLOYD, A. (Lawrence and Wishart, 1967) 'Until quite recently, in the printed collections of traditional song, there has been an almost complete expurgation of erotic detail.' Lloyd gives a fair account of collectors' ways, singers' self-censorship, and of what was collected.

The Merry Muses of Caledonia, BURNS, R. (W. H. Allen, 1965) What the right kind of collector collects, and restores.

The Age of Reason, PAINE, T. (Citadel Press. U.S.A. 1977) A beautifully clear, critical examination of the texts and beliefs of the Old and New Testaments.

Moses and Monotheism, FREUD, S. (Hogarth Press, 1951) Where the Old Testament comes from. By psychology, history, and text, Freud shows that Jewish monotheism came from the 'heretic' Pharaoh, Akhnaten; and Moses, himself, was an Egyptian.

Our Pagan Christmas, CONDON, R. J. (G. W. Foote, 1974) This tells how the story of the birth of Jesus was fabricated from the mythical histories of pagan gods; together with the origins and meanings of Yule-tide customs.

Apocalypse, LAWRENCE, D. H. (Penguin, 1974) 'A pagan substratum is overwritten by Jewish apocalyptists, then extended, and finally rewritten by the Jewish Christian, John.' Basically, the Gospel is the imagined triumph of the Christian 'meek', who are possessed with envy and hatred of all the 'unmeek'.

Etruscan Places, Lawrence, D. H. (Penguin, 1950) His understanding of pre-Roman paganism, and his interpretation of the paintings and symbols in the Etruscan tombs.

The Plumed Serpent, LAWRENCE, D. H. (Penguin, 1970) How a new paganism might be, its ceremonies and values; and how it might come about.

The Way of All Flesh, BUTLER, S. (Everyman's Library, Dent, 1968) A novel-autobiography of freeing oneself from parents, school, university, Church, and sexual repression—i.e. the complete book!

Index of First Lines

Restored Rhymes

Restored Carols